Nikon D7100:
From
Snapshots to
Great Shots

John Batdorff

Peachpit Press

Nikon D7100: From Snapshots to Great Shots
John Batdorff

Peachpit Press
www.peachpit.com

To report errors, please send a note to errata@peachpit.com
Peachpit Press is a division of Pearson Education

Project Editor: Susan Rimerman
Developmental/Copy Editor: Peggy Nauts
Production Editor: Rebecca Winter
Proofreader: Elaine Merrill
Composition: Danielle Foster
Indexer: James Minkin
Cover Design: Aren Straiger
Cover Image: John Batdorff
Interior Design: Riezebos Holzbaur Design Group

ISBN-13: 978-0-321-93496-3
ISBN–10:   0-321-93496-2

9 8 7 6 5 4 3 2 1

Printed and bound in the United States of America

ACKNOWLEDGMENTS

If life has taught me anything in the past few years, it's that you're only as strong as the people with whom you surround yourself. To Anna, my daughter, we just get each other and I suspect we always will. Oh, and quit filling my iPod with Taylor Swift and I'll quit subjecting you to Leonard Cohen. Staci, my love, you're a rock and I would be lost without you. Your sense of direction is unmatched, along with your taste in men! Seriously, I love you both more than words can express. Thank you for always being there for me.

A special thanks to Peggy Nauts for cleaning up my copy and removing my foot from my mouth on more than one occasion. You're a rock star.

Susan Rimerman, my editor, this is our fourth book together, so I think this officially makes us book buddies. Thanks for your encouragement and your relentless bluntness—I love it!

To the Peachpit crew, thank you for all your support throughout the years. You've become like family. Finally, to all of you who have bought this book, enjoy your new camera and remember to have fun! If you ever have any questions, feel free to contact me on my blog.

The camera used while writing this *From Snapshots to Great Shots* book was generously provided by B&H Photo.

www.bhphotovideo.com

Contents

Introduction

Welcome to your new camera! I know how exciting it is to get a new piece of equipment, so let me start off by telling you a little bit about how this book is going to help you master that new camera. You already know that you have *the* guide to your camera because it came right in the box: the owner's manual. But don't worry, *Nikon D7100: From Snapshots to Great Shots* is not a rehash of the manual. It is a resource to teach photographic concepts using the wonderful technology of the D7100, with instructional photos and insights from my own work as a professional photographer. I have put together a short Q&A to help you get a better understanding of just what it is that you can expect from this book.

Q: IS EVERY CAMERA FEATURE GOING TO BE COVERED?

A: Nope, just the ones I think you need to know about in order to start taking great photos. As I said, you already own a great resource that covers every feature of your camera: the owner's manual. (I know, we all hate reading manuals—we want to grab our new camera and start shooting. But if you look at your manual more closely, you'll realize it can actually help you.) A book that just rephrases this information would have been a waste of your time and money. What I did want to write about was how to harness certain camera features to benefit your photography. As you read through this book, you will also see references to specific pages in your owner's manual that are related to the topic being discussed. For example, in Chapter 6 the AE-L button is discussed, but there is more information available on this feature in the manual. I cover the function that applies to our specific needs and give you the page numbers in the manual to explore this function further.

Q: SO IF I ALREADY OWN THE MANUAL, WHY DO I NEED THIS BOOK?

A: The manual does a pretty good job of telling you how to use a feature or turn it on in the menus, but it doesn't necessarily tell you why and when you should use it. If you really want to improve your photography, you need to know the whys and the whens to put all of those great camera features to use. To that extent, the manual just isn't going to cut it. It is, however, a great resource on the camera's features, and for that reason I treat it like a companion to this book. You already own it, so why not get something of value from it?

Q: WHAT CAN I EXPECT TO LEARN FROM THIS BOOK?

A: My hope is that you will learn how to take great photographs. My goal, and the reason the book is laid out the way it is, is to guide you through the basics of photography as they relate to different situations and scenarios. By using the features of your D7100 and this book, you will learn about aperture, shutter speed, ISO, lens selection, depth of field, and many other photographic concepts. You will also find plenty of large full-page photos that include shooting data and comments from me so you can see how all of the photography fundamentals come together to make great images. Meanwhile, you will be learning how your camera works and how to apply its functions and features to your photography.

Q: DO I REALLY NEED TO DO THE ASSIGNMENTS?

A: In the shooting assignments, at the end of the chapters, I give you some suggestions on how you can apply the lessons of the chapter to help reinforce everything you just learned. Can I make you do them? No, but let's face it—using the camera is much more fun than reading about it, so the assignments are a way of taking a little break after each chapter, having some fun, and trying out your new chops.

Q: SHOULD I READ THE BOOK STRAIGHT THROUGH, OR CAN I SKIP AROUND FROM CHAPTER TO CHAPTER?

A: Here's the easy answer: yes and no. No, skipping around the whole time isn't the best idea, because the first four chapters give you the basic information that you need to know about your camera. These are the building blocks of using the D7100. After that, yes, you can move around the book as you see fit, because the following chapters are written to stand on their own as guides to specific types of photography or shooting situations. So you can bounce from portraits to landscapes and then maybe to a little action photography. It's all about your needs and how you want to address them. Or, you can read the book straight through. The choice is up to you.

Q: IS THAT IT?

A: One last thought before you dive into the first chapter. My goal in writing this book has been to give you a resource that will help you create great photographs with your Nikon D7100. Learning the basics is vital, but playing with them is what makes the photographer. Photography, like most things, takes time to master and requires practice. It has been a part of my life since I got my first Kodak 110 when I was seven years old, and I am still learning. Always remember, it's not the camera but the person using it who makes beautiful photographs. Have fun, make mistakes, and then learn from them. In no time, I'm sure you will transition from someone who takes nice snapshots to a photographer who makes great shots.

1

ISO 100
1/500 sec.
f/11
18mm lens

The D7100 Top 12 List

TWELVE TIPS TO MAKE YOUR SHOOTING MORE PRODUCTIVE RIGHT OUT OF THE BOX

Whenever I get a new camera, the first thing I do is grab the battery and the memory card and start shooting. What I should be doing is taking the extra time and reading the manual, but that's not much fun. Instead, I thought, why not make a chapter for people like me who can't wait to start taking images but don't want to feel guilty about not setting up their camera first? Here are 12 things you can do right now that are going to make your experience with your shiny new D7100 a ton better, from turning on the audible chirp for focusing to getting a feel for ISO settings, white balance settings, image review, focus settings, and several other custom functions that will help you right now. That doesn't mean I want you to skip over the other nine chapters, because they're filled with some really good tips, but this is a great starting point.

The D7100 is different from previous models in that many of the controls we use every day are available with a few clicks of a button. You no longer have to drill through two or three menus to make simple adjustments. But don't worry, for those of you who love menus, they're still there. I'll briefly discuss how to adjust settings using the buttons and then discuss some of the custom menu options for those of you looking to tweak your camera a bit.

PORING OVER THE PICTURE

CAMERA FRONT

A AF-assist illuminator
B Sub-command dial
C Depth of Field Preview button
D Function button
E Flash mode button

F Infrared receiver
G Bracketing button
H Lens mounting mark
I Lens Release button
J Focus mode selector and AF button

CAMERA BACK

A   Delete button
B   Playback button
C   Menu button
D   White Balance/Help/Protect button
E   Qual Button/ Zoom in/ Image Quality
F   ISO button/Zoom out/ ISO sensitivity
G   I Button
H   Monitor/LCD

I   Info button
J   Speaker
K   Live View selector with LV button
L   Focus Lock selector
M   Multi-selector with OK button
N   Main Command dial
O   AE/AF Lock button
P   Diopter Adjustment control

CAMERA TOP

A	Release Mode dial	G	Power switch
B	Mode dial	H	Shutter release button
C	Mode dial lock release	I	Exposure Compensation button
D	Release Mode dial lock release	J	Stereo microphone
E	Meter/Format button	K	Accessory shoe
F	Movie Record button	L	Control panel

CAMERA SIDE

A Microphone connector
B Headphone connector
C USB connector

D HDMI mini connector (Type C)
E Accessory terminal

1. SET THE CORRECT WHITE BALANCE

Color balance correction is the process of rendering accurate colors in your final image. Most people don't even notice that light has different color characteristics because the human eye automatically adjusts to different color temperatures— so quickly, in fact, that everything looks correct in a matter of milliseconds.

When color film ruled the world, photographers would select which film to use depending on what their light source was going to be. The most common film was balanced for daylight, but you could also buy film that was color balanced for tungsten light sources. Most other lighting situations had to be handled by using color filters over the lens. This process was necessary for the photographer's final image to show the correct color balance of a scene.

Luckily, you don't need to have a deep understanding of color temperatures to control your camera's white balance (**Figures 1.1** and **1.2**). The choices are given to you in terms that are easy to relate to and that will make things pretty simple.

Do I really need to change my white balance? I always answer this question by stating that if you're a RAW file shooter, then it depends on your workflow. I shoot strictly in RAW format, which allows me to change the white balance at any time in post-processing. However, I find setting my white balance to the correct setting in the field helps cut down on post-processing time. If you're a JPEG shooter, then the answer is an easy "yes, change the white balance!" As a JPEG shooter you'll want the camera to make the best possible color rendition, so having your white balance properly set will help the camera make the appropriate adjustments. But when in doubt, use auto.

FIGURE 1.1
This image is the result of making a mistake and picking the wrong white balance.

FIGURE 1.2
Here we have the correct white balance.

Your white balance choices are:

- **Auto:** The default setting for your camera. It is also the setting used by all of the automatic scene modes (see Chapter 3).

- **Incandescent:** Appropriate for any occasion when you are using regular household-type bulbs for your light source. Tungsten is a very warm light source and will result in a yellow-orange cast if you don't correct for it.

- **Fluorescent:** Gets rid of the green-blue cast that can result from using regular fluorescent lights as your dominant light source. Some fluorescent lights are actually balanced for daylight, which will allow you to use the Daylight white balance setting.

- **Direct Sunlight:** Most often used for general sunlit shooting.

- **Flash:** Used whenever you're employing the built-in flash or an external flash connected via the hot shoe. You should select this white balance to adjust for the slightly cooler light that comes from using a flash. (The hot shoe is the small bracket located on the top of your camera that rests just above the eyepiece. This bracket is used for attaching a more powerful flash to the camera.)

- **Cloudy:** The choice for overcast or very cloudy days. This and the Shade setting will eliminate the blue colorcast from your images.

- **Shade:** Used when working in shaded areas where sunlight is the dominant light source.

- **Pre:** Indicates that you are using a customized white balance that is adjusted for a particular light source. This option can be adjusted using an existing photo you have taken or by taking a picture of something white or gray in the scene.

Your camera has three different "zones" of shooting modes to choose from. These are located on the Mode dial, which separates your choices into automatic scene modes, effects, and what I refer to as the professional modes. None of the automatic scene or effects modes, which are chosen by turning the Mode dial to Scene or to Effects and then rotating the Command dial to choose a particular mode, allow for much customization, including white balance. The professional modes, defined by the letter symbols M, A, S, P, U1, and U2, allow for much more control by the photographer (**Figure 1.3**).

FIGURE 1.3
The camera's shooting modes are divided into the automatic scene modes, effects (special effects), and the professional modes (M, A, S, P, U1, and U2).

SETTING THE WHITE BALANCE

1. After turning on or waking the camera, select one of the professional shooting modes such as P (you can't select white balance when using any of the automatic modes).

2. Press and hold the WB button (**A**) on the back of the camera to activate White Balance, visible on the control panel or rear LCD.

3. While pressing the WB button, use your thumb to rotate the main Command dial to the appropriate White Balance setting, and release it to make your selection (**B**).

A

B

2. TURN OFF THE AUTO ISO SETTING

The ISO setting in your camera allows you to choose the level of sensitivity of the camera sensor to light. The ability to change this sensitivity is one of the biggest advantages to using a digital camera. In the days of film cameras, you had to choose the ISO by film type. This meant that if you wanted to shoot in lower light, you had to replace the film in the camera with one that had a higher ISO. So not only did you have to carry different types of film, but you also had to remove one roll from the camera to replace it with another, even if you hadn't used up the current roll. Now all you have to do is go to your information screen and select the appropriate ISO.

Having this flexibility is powerful, but just as with the JPEG quality setting, the ISO setting has a direct bearing on the quality of the final image. The higher the ISO, the more digital noise the image will contain. Since our goal is to produce high-quality photographs, it is important to get control over all of the camera settings and bend them to our will. When you turn your camera on for the first time, the ISO will be set to Auto. This means that the camera is determining how much light is available and will choose what it believes is the correct ISO setting. Since you want to use the lowest ISO possible, you will need to turn this setting off and manually select the appropriate ISO.

Which ISO you choose depends on your level of available or ambient light. For sunny days or very bright scenes, use a low ISO, such as 100. As the level of light is reduced, raise the ISO level. Cloudy days or indoor scenes might require you to use ISO 400 (**Figure 1.4**). Low-light scenes, such as when you are shooting at night, will mean you need to bump up that ISO to as high as 1600. The thing to remember is to shoot with the lowest setting possible for maximum quality.

FIGURE 1.4
View the control panel to see the selected ISO.

The D7100 has the ability to shoot at a very high ISOs with very little noise, but I prefer to have direct control over those ISO settings, so I turn off Auto ISO. There are a few situations, however, where I would turn the feature back on, which I discuss in Chapter 5. But for now, let's review how to turn Auto ISO off.

SETTING THE ISO

Press and hold the ISO button on the back of the camera while rotating the main Command dial to select ISO Sensitivity based on available light, and release the button when you have made your selection.

NOISE

Noise is the enemy of digital photography, but it has nothing to do with the loudness of your camera operation. It is a term that refers to the electronic artifacts that appear as speckles in your image. Back in the days of film we would have simply called the image "grainy." Digital noise appears in darker shadow areas and is a result of the camera trying to amplify the signal to produce visible information. The more the image needs to be amplified—by raising the sensitivity through higher ISO—the greater the amount of noise there will be. To avoid digital noise, try to use a low ISO whenever possible.

You should know that the Auto ISO option is enabled as a default only when you use one of the automatic scene modes. When you use one of the professional modes (M, A, S, and P; we'll discuss these in Chapter 4), the Auto ISO feature will be automatically turned off. If you wish to use Auto ISO in one of these modes, you must activate it and set the auto parameters in the Shooting menu. If you plan on shooting with the Auto mode, you cannot turn off the Auto ISO option at all.

3. SET YOUR IMAGE QUALITY

Your new D7100 has a number of Image Quality settings to choose from, and depending on your needs, you can adjust them accordingly.

This is probably one of the most important setting adjustments you can make. Most professional photographers shoot using RAW file format because it gives them the greatest control over their images. Now, if RAW is a new term for you and you have no experience in post-processing applications like Adobe's Lightroom or Apple's Aperture, then I recommend holding off on selecting this setting for now.

If you're familiar with RAW, then I highly suggest you select that option now.

For non-RAW shooters, we will be focusing in on the JPEG option. JPEG is a format that has been around since 1994 and is widely accepted. Most of your photos that are e-mailed or uploaded to social network sites, like Facebook, are JPEG images. Moreover, most printing services such as Walgreens, Kodak, Shutterfly, and Mpix use JPEG.

The JPEG file format compresses your image before final storage on your memory card, meaning the camera, not you, is applying all of the image processing first. Image processing involves such factors as sharpening, color adjustment, contrast adjustment, noise reduction, and so on. Many photographers prefer to use the RAW file format to get greater control over the image processing. We will take a closer look at this in Chapter 2, but for now let's just make sure that we are using the best-quality JPEG possible.

The D7100 has nine settings for the JPEG format. There are three settings each for Large, Medium, and Small image sizes. These settings (Basic, Normal, and Fine) represent image compression. The Large, Medium, and Small settings determine the actual physical size of your image in pixels. Let's work with the highest-quality setting possible.

1. Press and hold the Qual button on the bottom left of the camera while rotating the main Command dial to select the Fine Image Quality setting (**A**). You can view the changes on the LCD screen on the back of the camera by pressing the Info button to activate the monitor. Or, my preferred method, you can view the changes in the control panel on the top right of the camera (**B**).

2. Then, while still holding down the Qual button on the left, rotate the Sub-command dial with your right finger to choose the file setting Large, which selects the largest image size available.

3. Release the Qual button when you have made your selection.

4. If you've set up your camera properly it should read L Fine in the control panel on the top of the camera.

 A

 B

As you will see when scrolling through the quality settings, the higher the quality, the fewer pictures you will be able to fit on your card. If you have an 8 GB memory card, the quality setting we have selected will allow you to shoot about 500 photographs before you fill up your card. I always try to choose quality over quantity.

Manual Callout

For a complete chart that shows the Image Quality settings with the number of possible shots for each setting, turn to page 348 in your user manual.

4. SET THE APPROPRIATE IMAGE AREA

One of the most interesting new features of the D7100 is the ability to change the camera's crop factor. This camera has a standard crop size of DX 24 x 16. You can change that setting to get some additional reach by increasing the crop factor to 1.3 times the standard, or 18 x 16.

The 1.3 DX crop has four main benefits. First, it gives you a faster frame advance rate of 7 frames per second when in JPEG/12-bit NEF RAW mode. Second, it creates a telephoto effect without the need for changing lenses because it instantly increases the reach of your lens by 1.3. Third, because the viewable area is smaller, the camera records less information. Thus, the recorded file sizes are smaller. For instance, a standard DX 12-bit RAW file is 22.7 MB, and a 1.3 DX crop 12-bit RAW file is only 15.1 MB in comparison. Lastly, because the 1.3 crop image area is smaller, nearly all 51 AF points are able to saturate the viewable area, allowing for a very selective focus.

Now, I know all of this sounds really great, but my personal opinion is that this feature will be loved by those who find a special use for it and neglected by most. I can see some sports photography enthusiasts using this feature when they want better AF coverage and when a 1-frame-per-second increase in shutter speed is beneficial. I also found that when I was trying to get an image of a bird that was out of my reach, it helped me get closer without fumbling for a different lens. If I'd had to mess with changing lenses, I could have missed the image. However, for our purposes going forward, this will be the only place in the book where I'll address using the 1.3 crop, to avoid any unnecessary confusion. My suggestion is that if this is your first dSLR, or if this concept is new to you, practice using the standard DX frame size before experimenting with the 1.3 crop. As I will remind you throughout this book, experimentation is key to your growth, so come back to this section and try out the feature once you become familiar with your camera—give it a test drive with your sports, macro, or wildlife photography.

Here's how to turn the feature on and off:

1. Turn your camera on and press the *i* button (**A**).

2. Next, using your Multi-selector, select Image Area and press OK (**B**).

3. Select 1.3x (18 x 12) using your Multi-selector and press OK (**C**).

A

Remember, the 1.3 crop will remain even if you turn the camera on and off. To change the crop back to its default, simply follow steps 1 and 2, and then select DX (24 x 16).

5. SET YOUR FOCUS POINT AND MODE

The Nikon focusing system is well known for its speed and accuracy. The automatic focus modes will give you a ton of flexibility in your shooting. There is, however, one small problem inherent with any focusing system. No matter how intelligent it is, the camera is looking at all of the subjects in the scene and noting which is closest to the camera. It then uses this information to determine where the proper focus point should be. It has no way of knowing what your main emphasis is, so it is using a "best guess" system. To eliminate this factor, you should set the camera to single-point focusing so that you can ensure that you are focusing on the most important feature in the scene.

The camera has 51 separate focus points to choose from. They are arranged in a grid, but I always like to start by selecting the focus point in the center. Once you have become more familiar with the focus system, you can experiment with the other points, as well as the automatic point selection.

You should also change the focus mode to AF-S so that you can focus on your subject and then recompose your shot while holding that point of focus.

1. To choose a single point of focus, wake the camera (if necessary) by lightly pressing the shutter release button.

2. Press and hold the AF-mode button, on the front of the camera near the lens, using your left thumb. Now rotate the main Command dial to select AF-S (Single-servo AF) mode. This mode is used for photographing stationary objects but can be used in some motion shots as well. Next, rotate your Sub-command dial to select your AF-area mode; in this case we want Single-point AF, represented by the letter S.

The camera is now ready for single focusing. You will know if your subject is in focus by pressing the shutter button halfway while watching for the in-focus indicator to appear in the viewfinder. (Please review page 37 of your manual for a visual.) To focus on your subject and then recompose your shot, just place the focus point in the viewfinder on your subject, depress the shutter release button halfway until the in-focus indicator appears, and without letting up on the shutter button, recompose your shot and then press the shutter button all the way down to make your exposure (**Figure 1.5**).

FIGURE 1.5
Using the center single focus point in AF-S mode allows you to focus on your subject in the center, then recompose your photograph.

6. MANUAL FOCUS

As good as the Nikon autofocus system is, there are times when it just isn't doing the job for you. Often this has to do with how you would like to compose a scene and where the actual point of focus should be. This can be especially true when you are using the camera on a tripod, where you can't prefocus and then recompose before shooting. In some low-light situations, your camera may find it difficult to focus the lens even with the assistance of the AF-assist illuminator. To remedy this problem, you will need to manually focus the lens. I am only going to cover the kit lens that came with my D7100 (the 18–105mm VR), so if you have purchased a different lens be sure to check its accompanying instruction manual.

On the 18–105mm kit lens, you simply need to slide the switch located at the base of the lens (located on the lens barrel near the body of the camera) from the A setting to the M setting (**Figure 1.6**). You can now turn the focus ring at the end of the lens to set your focus. Now that you're in manual focus mode, the camera will not give you any notification when you have correctly focused. If you are using a non-AF-S lens, then you will need to move the focus mode switch on the barrel of the camera to M as well as the focus mode selector to M.

We'll cover more manual focus situations in greater detail in future chapters.

FIGURE 1.6
Slide the focus switch on the lens to the M position to manually focus.

7. REVIEW YOUR SHOTS

One of the greatest features of a digital camera is its ability to give us instant feedback. By reviewing your images on the camera's LCD, you can instantly tell if you got your shot. This visual feedback allows you to make adjustments on the fly. However, the D7100 ships with the Image Review feature turned off. If you want instant feedback on your images, then you should consider turning this feature back on.

1. Highlight Image Review in your Playback menu using the Multi-selector and press OK (**A**).

2. Next, using your Multi-selector, highlight the On option and press OK (**B**).

A

B

After this feature is turned on, when you first press the shutter release button, your camera quickly processes your shot and then displays the image on the LCD. The default setting for that display is four seconds. Four seconds works for me, but if you want to increase the amount of time you have to view a shot, such as up to 10 seconds, you can do that, using the following steps.

1. Go to the Custom Setting menu and select C Timers/AE Lock (**A**).

2. Choose C4 Monitor Off Delay (**B**).

3. Select Image Review and choose your preferred review time (**C**).

Two display modes give you different amounts of information while reviewing your photos. The default view (**Figure 1.7**) simply displays your image along with its filename, date, time, and image quality.

FIGURE 1.7
This is the standard view when reviewing images on your camera's monitor.

REVIEW EVEN MORE IMAGE DETAILS

FIGURE 1.8

This display mode gives you much more information.

To get more visual feedback, press the Multi-selector up to display the second display view, called Overview Data (**Figure 1.8**). This view mode not only displays the same information as the default view, but also includes aperture, shutter speed, lens length, white balance, exposure compensation, shooting mode, ISO, white balance setting, picture style, quality setting, any compensation settings, the active color space, picture control, and the D-Lighting setting. The other noticeable item will be the histogram, which gives you important feedback on the luminance values in your image (more on this below, in "The Value of the Histogram" sidebar).

You probably won't want to use this display option as your default review setting because the image thumbnail is so small, but if you are trying to figure out what settings you used or if you want to review the histogram, you now have all of this great information available.

Other display options are available, but they must be turned on using the Playback menu under Playback Display Options (**Figure 1.9**). With this menu choice you can add display modes such as Highlights, RGB histograms (**Figure 1.10**), and additional camera data (**Figure 1.11**). I personally don't use the RGB Histogram and Shooting Data settings because they don't offer me any visual information that I find critical during a photo session. I do, however, always have the Highlights option turned on so that I can make sure I'm not clipping any information from my image highlights.

FIGURE 1.9

Display mode options: Here's where you need to choose the image information you want displayed when reviewing an image during playback.

FIGURE 1.10
The RGB histogram display mode: If you're interested in monitoring the histogram of your images' color channels, select this option.

FIGURE 1.11
The Data display mode: Select this option if you wish to display focal length, exposure, lens info, and more.

DELETING IMAGES

Deleting or erasing images is a fairly simple process, which is covered on page 40 of your manual. To quickly get on your way, simply press the Image Playback button and use the Multi-selector to find the picture that you want to delete. Then press the Trash button, located on the back of the camera to the left of the eyepiece. When you see the confirmation screen, simply press the Trash button once again to complete the process.

Caution: Once you have deleted an image, it is gone for good. Make sure you don't want it before you drop it in the trash.

8. WHERE'S THE BEEP? CUSTOM FOCUSING OPTIONS

The D7100 is known for being ultra quiet. When I received my camera from the factory, I noticed there was no beep when I focused in on an image. The camera had shipped to me with the focus confirmation beep turned off. Some of you will like having this feature off and some of you, like me with my aging eyesight, enjoy hearing that little confirmation beep telling us that the lens is in focus. Often I'm moving very quickly, and just hearing a beep that says everything is in focus is reassuring. Here's how you can turn the beep back on and select a volume.

1. Press the Menu button.

2. Choose Custom Setting Menu.

3. Select D Shooting/Display.

4. Choose D1 Beep.

   • Select Volume and Pitch.

   • Click OK.

Focus Point Wrap—Turn this feature on and you'll save your thumb from doing a lot of clicking when you're working from opposite ends of the AF points.

1. Press the Menu button.

2. Select Custom Setting Menu.

3. Choose A Autofocus.

4. Choose A5 Focus Point Wrap Around.

   • Select On.

AF-Assist Illuminator—The D7100 is equipped with an autofocus illuminator. Basically, a light comes on when the camera is trying to focus in the dark. It's similar to a red-eye light but serves a totally different purpose. I am not a fan of this function, but you may like it. I don't recommend it for low-light portraits because the flashing light bothers some people's eyes. If you want to turn this function off, either all the time or only for low-light portraits, here is how you do that.

1. Press the Menu button.

2. Select Custom Setting Menu.

3. Choose A Autofocus.

4. Select A7 Built in AF-assist Illuminator.

   • Select Off.

   • Press OK.

THE VALUE OF THE HISTOGRAM

Simply put, histograms are two-dimensional representations of your images in graph form. There are two histograms that you should be concerned with: the luminance and the color histograms. Luminance is referred to in your manual as "brightness" and is most valuable when evaluating your exposures. In **Figure 1.12**, you see what looks like a mountain range. The graph represents the entire tonal range that your camera can capture, from the whitest whites to the blackest blacks. The left side represents black, and all the way to the right side represents white. The peaks indicate the number of pixels that contain those luminance levels (a tall peak in the middle means your image contains a large amount of medium-bright pixels).

Looking at this figure, it is initially hard to determine where all of the ranges of light and dark areas are and how much of each I have. If I look at the histogram, I can see that the largest peak of the graph is in the middle and trails off as it reaches the edges. In most cases, you would look for this type of histogram, indicating that you captured the entire range of tones, from dark to light, in your image. Knowing that is fine, but here is where histogram information really gets useful.

A histogram that has a spike or peak riding up the far left or right side of the graph means that you are clipping detail from your image. In essence, you are trying to record values that are either too dark or too light for your sensor to accurately record. This is usually an indication of over- or underexposure. It also means that you need to correct your exposure so that the important details will not record as solid black or white pixels (which is what happens when clipping occurs).

At times, however, some clipping is acceptable. If you are photographing a scene where the sun will be in the frame, you can expect to get some clipping because the sun is just too bright to hold any detail. Likewise, if you are shooting something that has true blacks in it— think coal in a mine shaft at midnight—there are most certainly going to be some true blacks with no detail in your shot. The main goal is to ensure that you aren't clipping any "important" visual information, and that is achieved by keeping an eye on your histogram.

Take a look at **Figure 1.13**. The histogram displayed at the bottom left of the image shows a heavy skew toward the left with almost no part of the mountain touching the right side. This is a good example

FIGURE 1.12
This is a typical histogram, where the dark to light tones run from left to right. The black to white gradient above the graph demonstrates where the tones lie on the graph and would not appear above your camera histogram display.

of what an underexposed image histogram looks like. Now look at **Figure 1.14** and compare the histogram for the image that was correctly exposed. Notice that even though there are distinct peaks on the graph, there is a fairly even distribution across the entire histogram.

FIGURE 1.13
This image is about two stops underexposed. Notice the histogram is skewed to the left.

FIGURE 1.14
This histogram reflects a correctly exposed image.

9. CUSTOM DISPLAY OPTIONS

Viewfinder Grid—I love a viewfinder grid. I think it's super handy when composing images and lining things up. Those of you familiar with the rule of thirds will recognize this grid.

1. Press the Menu button.
2. Select Custom Setting Menu.
3. Choose D Shooting/Display.
4. Choose D2 Viewfinder Grid Display.

   - Select On.
   - Press OK.

ISO Display—If you want to view what your current ISO is instead of how many images you have left to shoot until your card is full, then you'll want to turn this feature on. When I'm shooting I worry more about my ISO setting than about how many more pictures I can take, so I prefer to keep this feature on.

1. Press the Menu button.
2. Choose Custom Setting Menu.
3. Select D Shooting Display.
4. Select D3 ISO Display and Adjustment.

   - Choose Show ISO Sensitivity.
   - Press OK.

10. SHUTTER DELAY OPTIONS

Exposure Delay mode—This is a landscape photographer's dream. It's a great feature to activate if you don't have a remote or cable release for your camera. We all know that movement is bad when taking long exposures. This feature delays the shutter for one second after the shutter release button has been pressed. But what makes it even cooler is that it only works when your camera is in Mirror-up. I love this feature because otherwise I would need to use a self-timer, but the problem with a self-timer is that it's designed around getting people in front of the camera, so the shortest delay is still longer than I need when taking landscape shots. Exposure Delay is better than using the timer because there isn't such a long delay, but it achieves the same function as a cable release.

Exposure Delay mode

1. Press the Menu button.
2. Choose Custom Setting Menu.
3. Select D Shooting/Display.
4. Choose D10 Exposure Delay Mode.

   • Select either 1s, 2s, or 3s Delay and press OK.

Self-Timer Mode

1. Press the Menu button.
2. Choose Custom Setting Menu.
3. Select C Timers/AE Lock.
4. Choose C3 Self-Timer.

   • Select Self-Timer Delay (from 2 to 20 seconds).

11. OH, SHOOT! RESET OPTIONS

Don't you wish everything in life had a reset button? Well, the folks at Nikon have made it simple with the D7100. If at any time you want to reset the camera's shooting options, then all you need to do is press the ISO button and Exposure Compensation button (a green button is located next to each icon) simultaneously for two seconds (**Figure 1.15**). The control panel will turn off as it resets, indicating that the shooting options have been reset to their default. If you need to reset the Shooting menu or restore custom settings, then follow the steps below.

FIGURE 1.15
Press the ISO button and Exposure Compensation button simultaneously to reset shooting options.

1. To restore the Shooting menu to its default, go to the Shooting menu and select Reset Shooting Menu (**A**). Press OK and select Yes.

2. Finally, to restore your custom settings to their default values, go to the Custom Setting menu and select Reset Custom Settings (**B**). Press OK and select Yes.

A

B

12. HOLD YOUR CAMERA FOR PROPER SHOOTING

It's worth taking a few seconds to think about how you hold your camera. DSLR cameras are made to favor right-handed people. Grasp the camera body with your right hand. Most of the important camera controls are within easy reach. Create a stable base for your camera to rest on by placing the camera body on the up-facing palm of your left hand (**Figure 1.16**). Now you can curl your fingers around the lens barrel. By using the underhand grip, you keep your elbows close to your body. Pull them in to stabilize your shooting position. Also try to maintain proper upright posture. Leaning forward at the waist will begin to fatigue your back, neck, and arms. Finally, place your left foot in front of your right foot, and face your subject in a wide stance.

FIGURE 1.16
Here's the proper way to hold your camera to ensure sharp, blur-free images.

Chapter 1 Assignments

Let's begin our shooting assignments by setting up and using all of the elements of the Top 12 list. Even though I have yet to cover the professional shooting modes, you should set your camera to the P (Program) mode. This will allow you to interact with the various settings and menus that have been covered thus far.

Basic camera setup

Charge your battery to 100 percent. Next, using your newfound knowledge, set up your camera to address the following settings: Image Quality and Auto ISO.

Selecting the proper white balance

Take your camera outside into a daylight environment and then photograph the same scene using different white balance settings. Pay close attention to how each setting affects the overall colorcast of your images. Next, try moving inside and repeating the exercise while shooting in a tungsten lighting environment. Finally, find a fluorescent light source and repeat one more time.

Focusing with single point and AF-S

Change your camera setting so that you are focusing using single-point focus. Try using all of the different focus points to see how they work in focusing your scene. Then set your focus mode to AF-S and practice focusing on a subject and then recomposing before actually taking the picture. Try doing this with subjects at varying distances. Remember to turn Focus Wrap Around on.

Evaluating your pictures with the monitor

Set up your image display properties and then review some of your previous assignment images using the different display modes. Review your shooting information for each image and take a look at the histograms to see how the content of your photo affects the shape of the histograms.

Discovering the manual focus mode

Change your focus mode from Auto to Manual and practice a little manual focus photography. Get familiar with where the focus ring is and how to use it to achieve sharp images.

Get a grip: proper camera holding

This final assignment is something that you should practice every time you shoot: proper grip and stance for shooting with your camera. Use the described technique and then shoot a series of images. Then try shooting some with improper technique to compare the stability of the grip and stance.

Share your results with the book's Flickr group!
Join the group here: flickr.com/groups/nikond7100_fromsnapshotstogreatshots.

2

ISO 500
1/250 sec.
f/11
35mm lens

First Things First

A FEW THINGS TO KNOW AND DO BEFORE YOU BEGIN TAKING PICTURES

Now that we've covered the top 12 tips to get you up and shooting, we should probably take care of some other important details. You must become familiar with certain features of your camera before you can take full advantage of it. Additionally, we will take some steps to prepare the camera and memory card for use. So to get things moving, let's start off with something that you will definitely need before you can take a single picture: a memory card.

PORING OVER THE PICTURE

The snows of Kilimanjaro are legendary, but even when I summited Kili, in 2004, I never had the opportunity to see the mountain from a distance. It wasn't until my return trip a few years later that I was finally graced with the view that had eluded me during my climb.

Sunrise shots are all about getting up early. Generally I arrive on site in the dark to set up for the shot. Preparation and some good fortune can go a long way.

Using a neutral density filter allowed me to darken the sky while properly exposing the foreground.

Some months are better than others for viewing Kilimanjaro, so doing your research before traveling great distances can really aid in your success. Oh, and luck has a little something to do with it, too!

ISO 100
1/90 sec.
f/8
80mm lens

CHOOSING THE RIGHT MEMORY CARD

Selecting a memory card that is appropriate for your camera and your needs is a crucial step to avoiding problems in the future. Your new D7100 is equipped with two Secure Digital (SD) memory card slots (**Figure 2.1**).

If you have been using a point-and-shoot camera, chances are you already own an SD media card. Which brand of card you use is up to you, but here is some advice about choosing a memory card:

FIGURE 2.1
Make sure you select an SD card that has enough capacity to handle your photography needs.

- Capacity matters. At 29 megapixels, the D7100 will require a lot of storage space, especially if you shoot in the RAW or RAW+JPEG mode (more on this later in the chapter). You should definitely consider using a card with a storage capacity of at least 8 GB.

- Write speed is critical. Your Nikon D7100 can write to a card very quickly—that is, if the card is fast enough. Learn from my mistakes. You don't want to buy an inexpensive memory card that can't keep up with your camera's file write speed. Having a card that can't keep up can result in corrupted files as well as lost photo opportunities. Transfer speed is a key factor when shooting in Continuous Drive mode (see Chapter 5) or when recording video. If your card is not rated fast enough or doesn't have enough capacity, then you will be left in the dust. Here are some of Nikon's recommendations for your D7100.

- If you shoot video, or plan on shooting in Continuous mode, choose an SDHC card with a class 6 or faster write speed. The D7100 also supports the newest and fastest card, the SDXC, which has a faster transfer speed and larger capacity than the standard SDHC.

- Buy more than one card. If you have already purchased a memory card, consider getting another. You can quickly ruin your day of shooting by filling your card and then having to either erase shots or choose a lower-quality image format so that you can keep on shooting. Given that memory cards are relatively affordable, keeping a spare just makes good sense. Plus, the D7100 has two memory card slots for storage—but more about that later.

FORMATTING YOUR MEMORY CARD

Now that you have your card, let's talk about formatting for a minute. When you purchase any new SD card, you can pop it into your camera and start shooting right away—and probably everything will work as it should. However, what you should do first is format the card in the camera. This process allows the camera to set up the card to record images from your camera. Just as a computer hard drive must be formatted, formatting your card ensures that it is properly initialized. The card may work in the camera without first being formatted, but chances of failure down the road are much higher.

As a general practice, I always format new cards or cards that have been used in different cameras. I also reformat cards after I have downloaded my images and want to start a new shooting session. Note that you should always format your card in the camera, not your computer. Using the computer could render the card useless. You should also pay attention to the card manufacturer's recommendations in respect to moisture, humidity, and proper handling procedures. It sounds a little clichéd, but when it comes to protecting your images, every little bit helps.

A

B

HOW TO FORMAT A MEMORY CARD

1. Insert your memory card into the camera.

2. Press the Menu button and navigate to the Setup menu screen.

3. Use the Multi-selector on the back of the camera to highlight the Format Memory Card option and press OK (**A**).

4. Next you will have the option of formatting Slot 1 or Slot 2. Pick the appropriate card slot to format and click OK (**B**).

5. The next screen will show you a warning, letting you know that formatting the card will delete images (**C**). Select Yes and press OK.

6. The card is now formatted and ready for use.

C

UPDATING THE D7100'S FIRMWARE

I know that you want to get shooting, but having the proper firmware can affect the way the camera operates. It can fix problems as well as improve operation, so you should probably check it sooner rather than later.

Updating your camera's firmware is something that the manual omits, yet it can change the entire behavior of your camera's operating systems and functions. The firmware of your camera is the set of computer operating instructions that control how your camera functions. Updating it is a great way to not only fix little bugs but also gain access to new functionality. You will need to check out the information on the Nikon Download Center page (see below) to see if a firmware update is available and how it will affect your camera, but it is always a good idea to be working with the most up-to-date firmware version available.

Keep in mind, it is not uncommon for a new camera model to see several firmware upgrades within the first six months after its release, so check back frequently at first, then every so often during the lifetime of the camera or if you experience any unexplained problems with the camera.

CHECKING THE CAMERA'S CURRENT FIRMWARE VERSION NUMBER

1. Press the Menu button and then navigate to the Setup menu.

2. Use the Multi-selector on the back of the camera to highlight the Firmware Version option and press OK (**A**).

3. Take note of the current version number (**B**), and then check the Nikon website to see if you are using the current version.

A

B

UPDATING THE FIRMWARE FROM YOUR SD CARD

1. Download the firmware update file from the Nikon website. (You can find the file by going to the Download Current Firmware section of the Nikon Download Center page at nikonusa.com/Service-And-Support/Download-Center.page and locating the firmware update for your camera and computer operating system.)

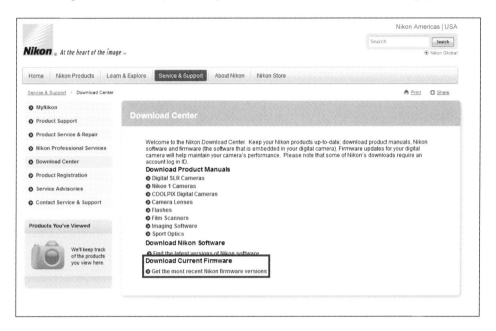

2. Once you have downloaded the firmware to your computer and extracted it, you will need to transfer the updated firmware to your SD card. However, prior to transferring the new firmware, you must first format your SD card in your camera and then transfer the firmware to the card.

3. Make sure your camera battery is fully charged. Insert the card into the camera and turn it on.

4. Follow the instructions for checking your camera's current firmware version, which are listed above, and you will now be able to update your firmware using the files located on the SD card.

At the time I finished writing this book, there were no firmware updates available for the D7100. After you check your camera firmware version and the Nikon site for updates, continue to check back periodically to see if updates become available.

CLEANING THE SENSOR

Cleaning camera sensors used to be a nerve-racking process that required leaving the sensor exposed to scratching and even more dust. Now cleaning the sensor is pretty much an automatic function. Every time you turn the camera on and off, you can instruct its sensor to vibrate to remove any dust particles that might have landed on it.

You have five choices for cleaning in the Setup menu: Clean at Startup, Clean at Shutdown, Clean at Startup/Shutdown, Cleaning Off, and Clean Now. I'm kind of obsessive when it comes to cleaning my sensor, so I like to have it set to Clean at Startup/Shutdown. This works nicely, since I make a habit of turning my camera off whenever I change my lenses. There are many schools of thought on this practice, but for the few seconds it takes I would rather not run the risk of damaging any electronics in the lens or camera.

Removing or changing a lens will leave the camera body open and susceptible to dust sneaking in. If you never change lenses, you shouldn't have too many dust problems. But the more often you change lenses, the more chances you are giving dust to enter the body. The camera sensor is an electrically charged device. This means that when the camera is turned on, there is a current running through the sensor. This electric current can create static electricity, which will attract small dust particles to the sensor area. For this reason, it is always a good idea to turn off the camera prior to removing a lens.

You should also consider having the lens mount facing down when changing lenses so that there is less opportunity for dust to fall into the inner workings of the camera. As long as you are turning the camera off while changing your lenses, the camera will automatically clean the sensor when you turn it back on.

Every now and then, there will just be a dust spot that is impervious to the shaking of the Auto Cleaning feature. This will require manual cleaning of the sensor by raising the mirror and opening the camera shutter. When you activate this feature, it will move everything out of the way, giving you access to the sensor so that you can use a blower or other cleaning device to remove the stubborn dust speck. The camera will need to be turned off after cleaning to allow the mirror to reset.

If you choose to manually clean your sensor, use a device that has been made to clean sensors (not a cotton swab from your medicine cabinet). There are dozens of commercially available devices such as brushes, swabs, and blowers that will clean the sensor without damaging it. To keep the sensor clean, always store the camera with a body cap or lens attached.

1. Press the Menu button, then navigate to the Setup menu.

2. Use the Multi-selector on the back of the camera to highlight the Clean Image Sensor option and press OK (**A**).

3. Pick Clean Now to clean the camera immediately or pick Clean at Startup/Shutdown to clean the camera whenever the camera is turned on or off (**B**). I prefer the latter setting. Once you've made your selection, press OK.

A

B

USING THE RIGHT FORMAT: RAW VS. JPEG

When shooting with your D7100, you have a choice of image formats that your camera will use to store the pictures on the memory card. JPEG is probably the format most familiar to anyone who has been using a digital camera.

There is nothing wrong with JPEG if you are taking casual shots. JPEG files are ready to use, right out of the camera. Why go through the process of adjusting RAW images of the kids opening presents when you are just going to e-mail them to Grandma? Also, for journalists and sports photographers who are shooting nine frames per second and who need to transmit their images across the wire, again, JPEG is just fine. So what is wrong with JPEG? Absolutely nothing—unless you care about having complete creative control over all of your image data.

JPEG is not actually an image format. It is a compression standard, and compression is where things go bad. When you have your camera set to JPEG—whether it is Fine, Normal, or Basic—you are telling the camera to process the image however it sees fit and then throw away enough image data to make it shrink into a smaller space. In doing so, you give up subtle image details that you will never get back in post-processing. That is an awfully simplified statement but still fairly accurate.

SO WHAT DOES RAW HAVE TO OFFER?

First and foremost, RAW images are like digital negatives and are typically not compressed. If they are compressed the camera uses lossless compression, which means there is no loss of actual image data. Note that RAW image files will require you to perform post-processing on your photographs. This is not only necessary, it is the reason that most photographers use it. You can use the software that came with your camera to process the RAW images (**Figure 2.2**), or for more control you can use an application like Adobe Lightroom or Apple's Aperture. I do all my own post-production in Adobe Lightroom. RAW images have a greater dynamic range than JPEG-processed images. This means that you can recover image details that just aren't available in JPEG-processed images.

FIGURE 2.2
ViewNX 2 can be used to import, edit, and print RAW files.

There is more color information in a RAW image because it is a 14-bit image, which means it contains more color information than a JPEG, which is almost always an 8-bit image. More color information means more to work with and smoother changes between tones. Regarding sharpening, a RAW image offers more control because you are the one who is applying the sharpening according to the effect you want to achieve. Once again, JPEG processing applies a standard amount of sharpening that you cannot change after the fact.

Finally, and most importantly, a RAW file is your negative. The file format is called nondestructive. Meaning, no matter what you do to it, you won't change it unless you save your file in a different format. This means that you can come back to that RAW file later and try different processing settings to achieve other results and never harm the original image. By comparison, if you make a change to your JPEG and accidentally save the file, guess what? You have a new original file, and you will never get back to that first image. That alone should make you sit up and take notice.

What I love about RAW is that, as technology changes, it allows me to go back and work the original file again and again without damaging or changing the "digital negative."

ADVICE FOR NEW RAW SHOOTERS

Don't give up on shooting RAW just because it means more work. Hey, it may take up more space on your card, but memory cards are not nearly as expensive as they used to be, and buying one 16 GB or two 8 GB cards will cost less than $20. Will it take more time to download? Yes, but good things come to those who wait. Don't worry about needing to purchase expensive software to work with your RAW files; you already own a program that will allow you to work with them. Nikon's ViewNX 2 software comes bundled in the box with your camera and gives you the ability to work directly on the RAW files and then output the enhanced results.

If you're unfamiliar with RAW format, my recommendation is to shoot in JPEG mode while you are using this book. This will allow you to quickly review your images and study the effects of the book's lessons. Once you have become comfortable with all of the camera features, you should switch to shooting in RAW mode so that you can start gaining more creative control over your image processing. After all, you took the photograph—shouldn't you be the one to decide how it looks in the end?

When photographers are discussing digital cameras, the term *image resolution* is often used to describe pixel resolution, or the number of pixels used to make an image. This can be displayed as a dimension, such as 6000 x 3368. This is the physical number of pixels in width and height of the image sensor. Resolution can also be referred to in megapixels (MP), such as 28.5 MP for a RAW 14-bit lossless compression. This number represents the number of total pixels on the sensor and is commonly used to describe the amount of image data that a digital camera can capture.

SHOOTING DUAL FORMATS

Your camera has the added benefit of being able to write two files for each picture you take, one in RAW and one in JPEG. This can be useful if you need a quick version to e-mail but want a higher-quality version for more advanced processing. You will notice that there is a dash (—) option at the beginning of the RAW and JPEG settings. If you don't want to shoot in both RAW and JPEG together, you must set one of the formats to the dash. If you have a RAW and JPEG setting selected, your camera willsave your images in both formats on your card.

Note that using both formats would require more space on the memory card. With the D7100 you have the option to record your RAW images on one memory card and the JPEGs on another. So if you have one large and one small memory card, you can designate the larger card to write the RAW files and the smaller card to write the JPEG files. This option will also give you a chance to experiment with RAW if you're unfamiliar with it and still have the security blanket of JPEG. You can also see the difference between the two and decide for yourself which file type you prefer. However, I recommend that you eventually use only one format or the other unless you have a specific need to shoot both.

SHOOTING IN RAW AND JPEG

1. Press and hold the Qual button on the back of the camera (**A**). While holding the Qual button, rotate the main Command dial with your right thumb until it shows RAW+Fine, RAW+Norm, or RAW+Basic (**B**).

2. You can then choose the size of the JPEG file by holding the Qual button and rotating the Sub-command dial with your right finger to choose S, M, or L for small, medium, or large JPEG (**C**).

3. Release the Qual button to make your final selection (see Chapter 1).

SAVING RAW AND JPEG FILES TO SEPARATE CARDS

1. To choose one memory card to record JPEG and the other RAW (**A**), press the Menu button on the back of the camera.

2. Use the Multi-selector to choose the Shooting menu.

3. Select the option Role Played by Card in Slot 2 and press OK (**B**).

4. Using the Multi-selector, choose RAW Slot 1 – JPEG Slot 2, and press OK to final-
   ize your selection (**C**).

You will notice when you are in the selection screen on the top display of the camera
that you will be able to see how much storage space each option will require on your SD
card. This is the number to the right of the screen. The RAW+Fine L option, which is the
one I use, will take up approximately 40 MB of space for each photograph you take.

LENSES AND FOCAL LENGTHS

If you ask most professional photographers what they believe to be their most critical
piece of photographic equipment, they will undoubtedly tell you that it is their lens.
The technology and engineering that goes into your camera is a marvel, but it isn't
worth a darn if it can't get the light from the outside onto the sensor. The D7100, as
a digital single lens reflex (dSLR) camera, uses the lens for a multitude of tasks, from
focusing on a subject to metering a scene to delivering and focusing the light onto
the camera sensor. The lens is also responsible for the amount of the scene that will
be captured (the frame). With all of this riding on the lens, let's take a more in-depth
look at the camera's eye on the world.

Lenses are composed of optical glass that is both concave and convex in shape. The
alignment of the glass elements is designed to focus the light coming in from the
front of the lens onto the camera sensor. The amount of light that enters the camera is also controlled by the lens, the size of the glass elements, and the aperture
mechanism within the lens housing. The quality of the glass used in the lens will
have a direct effect on how well the lens can resolve details and also the contrast

of the image (the ability to deliver great highlights and shadows). Most lenses now routinely include things like the autofocus motor and, in some cases, a vibration-reduction mechanism. If you bought the Nikon D7100 kit lens, then your 18–105mm lens is equipped with autofocus as well as vibration reduction.

There is one other aspect of the camera lens that is often the first consideration of the photographer: lens length. Lenses are typically divided into three or four groups depending on the field of view they deliver.

Wide-angle lenses cover a field of view from around 110 degrees to about 60 degrees (**Figure 2.3**). There is a tendency to get some distortion in your image when using extremely wide-angle lenses. This will be apparent toward the outer edges of the frame. As for which lenses would be considered wide angle, anything 35mm or smaller could be considered wide.

ISO 250
1/640 sec.
f/7.1
16mm lens

FIGURE 2.3
The 16mm lens setting provides a wide view of the scene but little detail in distant objects.
I photograph most of my landscape images with a wide-angle 16–35mm lens.

Wide-angle lenses can display a large depth of field, which allows you to keep the foreground and background in sharp focus. This makes them very useful for landscape photography. They also work well in tight spaces, such as indoors, where there isn't much elbow room available. They can be handy for large-group shots but aren't so great for close-up portrait work, due to the amount of distortion.

A *normal* lens has a field of view that is about 45 degrees and delivers approximately the same view as the human eye. The perspective feels very natural, and there is little distortion in objects. The normal lens for full-frame and 35mm cameras is the 50mm lens, but for the D7100 it is more in the neighborhood of a 35mm lens. Often I'll use a 50mm or an 85mm for street photography (**Figure 2.4**).

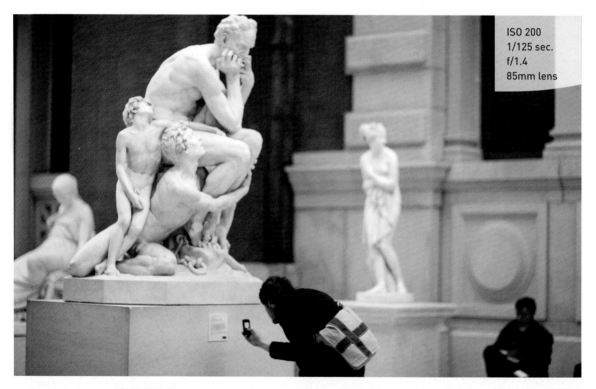

ISO 200
1/125 sec.
f/1.4
85mm lens

FIGURE 2.4
This image was photographed using an 85mm lens. I really enjoy observing people. I'm not sure why but this image just brings a smile to my face.

Long viewed as the "normal" lens for 35mm photography, the 50mm focal length can be considered somewhat of a telephoto lens on the D7100 because it has the same angle of view and magnification as an 80mm lens on a 35mm camera body. I find it to be the perfect lens to use for many portraits.

Normal focal length lenses are useful for photographing people and architecture and for most other general photographic purposes. They have very little distortion and offer a moderate range of depth of field (**Figure 2.5**).

Most longer focal length lenses are referred to as *telephoto* lenses. They can range in length from 135mm up to 800mm or longer and have a field of view that is about 35 degrees or smaller. These lenses have the ability to greatly magnify the scene, allowing you to capture details of distant objects, but the angle of view is sharply reduced. You will also find that you can achieve a much narrower depth of field. They suffer from something called distance compression, which means they make objects at different distances appear to be much closer together than they really are (**Figure 2.6**).

ISO 100
1/320 sec.
f/6.3
35mm lens

FIGURE 2.5
The 35mm or 50mm is often considered a great street-photography lens because of its compact size combined with large aperture.

ISO 1000
1/500 sec.
f/4.0
300mm lens

FIGURE 2.6
It would have been a little dangerous for me to get this close to a lion, so using a telephoto lens was key in getting this image from the Serengeti.

Telephoto lenses are most useful for wildlife and sports photography or any application where you just need to get closer to your subject. They can have a compressing effect—making objects look closer together than they actually are—and a very narrow depth of field when used at their widest apertures.

A *zoom* lens is a great compromise to carrying a bunch of single focal-length lenses (also referred to as prime lenses). They can cover a wide range of focal lengths because of the configuration of their optics. However, because it takes more optical elements to capture a scene at different focal lengths, the light must pass through more glass on its way to the image sensor. The more glass, the lower the quality of the image sharpness. The other sacrifice that is made is in aperture. Zoom lenses typically have smaller maximum apertures than prime lenses, which means they cannot achieve a narrow depth of field or work in lower-light levels without the assistance of image stabilization, a tripod, or higher ISO settings. (We'll discuss all this in more detail in later chapters.)

The D7100 can be purchased with the body only, but many folks will purchase it with a kit lens. The most common kit lens is the 18–105mm VR f/3.5–5.6. Throughout the book, I will occasionally make reference to lenses that are wider or more telephoto than these, because I have a multitude of lenses that I use for my photography. This doesn't mean that you have to run out and purchase more lenses. It just means that if you do this long enough, you are sure to accumulate additional lenses that will expand your ability to be even more creative with your photography.

WHAT IS EXPOSURE?

In order for you to get the most out of this book, I need to briefly discuss the principles of exposure. Without this basic knowledge, it will be difficult for you to move forward in improving your photography. There are many excellent books that have been written on exposure. I highly recommend *Exposure: From Snapshots to Great Shots* (Peachpit Press), by Jeff Revell. However, for our purposes I will just cover some of the basics. This will give you the essential tools to make educated decisions in determining how best to photograph a subject (**Figure 2.7**).

Exposure is the process whereby the light bouncing off a subject reflects through an opening in the camera lens for a defined period of time onto the camera sensor. The combination of the lens opening, shutter speed, and sensor sensitivity is used to achieve a proper exposure value (EV) for the scene. A relationship exists between these factors that is sometimes referred to as the exposure triangle.

ISO 400
1/100 sec.
f/2
85mm lens

FIGURE 2.7
This image was taken at dusk, and the light was changing very quickly. I needed to adjust the ISO several times to get the proper exposure.

At each point of the triangle lies one of the factors of exposure:

- **ISO:** Determines the sensitivity of the camera sensor. ISO stands for the International Organization for Standardization, but the acronym is used as a term to describe the sensitivity of the camera sensor to light. The higher the sensitivity, the less light is required for a good exposure. These values are a carryover from the days of traditional color and black-and-white films.

- **Aperture:** Also referred to as the f-stop, this determines how much light passes through the lens at once.

- **Shutter Speed:** Controls the length of time that light is allowed to hit the sensor.

Here's how it works. The camera sensor has a level of sensitivity that is determined by the ISO setting. To get a proper exposure—not too much, not too little—the lens needs to adjust the aperture diaphragm (the size of the lens opening) to control the volume of light entering the camera. Then the shutter is opened for a relatively short period of time to allow the light to hit the sensor long enough for it to record on the sensor.

ISO numbers for the D7100 start at 100 and then double in sensitivity as you double the number. So 200 is twice as sensitive as 100. The camera can be set to use one-half- or one-third-stop increments, but for ISO just remember that the base numbers double: 100, 200, 400, 800, and so on. You can also use a wide variety of shutter speeds. The speeds on the D7100 range from as long as 30 seconds to as short as 1/8000 of a second. When using the camera, you will not see the 1 over the number, so you will need to remember that anything shorter than a second will be a fraction.

Typically, you will be working with a shutter speed range from around 1/30 of a second to about 1/2000, but these numbers will change depending on your circumstances and the effect that you are trying to achieve. The lens apertures will vary slightly depending on which lens you are using. This is because different lenses have different maximum apertures. The typical apertures that are at your disposal are f/3.5, f/4, f/4.5, f/5.6, f/6.3, f/7.1, f/8, f/9, f/10, f/11, f/13, f/14, f/16, f/18, and f/22.

When it comes to exposure, a change to any one of these factors requires changing one or more of the other two. This is referred to as reciprocal change. If you let more light in the lens by choosing a larger aperture opening, you will need to shorten the amount of time the shutter is open. If the shutter is allowed to stay open for a longer period of time, the aperture needs to be smaller to restrict the amount of light coming in.

HOW IS EXPOSURE CALCULATED?

We now know about the exposure triangle—ISO, shutter speeds, and aperture—so it's time to put all three together to see how they relate to one another and how you can change them as needed.

STOP

You will hear the term *stop* thrown around all the time in photography. It relates back to the f-stop, which is a term used to describe the aperture opening of your lens. When you need to give some additional exposure, you might say that you are going to "add a stop." This doesn't just equate to the aperture; it could also be used to describe the shutter speed or even the ISO. So when your image is too light or dark or you have too much movement in your subject, you will probably be changing things by a "stop" or two.

When you point your camera at a scene, the light reflecting off your subject enters the lens and is allowed to pass through to the sensor for a period of time, as dictated by the shutter speed. The amount and duration of the light needed for a proper exposure depends on how much light is being reflected and how sensitive the sensor is. To figure this out, your camera uses a built-in light meter that looks through the lens and measures the amount of light. That level is then calculated against the sensitivity of the ISO setting and an exposure value is rendered. Here is the tricky part: There is no single way to achieve a perfect exposure because the f-stop and shutter speed can be combined in different ways to allow the same amount of exposure. See, I told you it was tricky.

Here is a list of reciprocal settings that would all produce the same exposure result. Let's use the "sunny 16" rule, which states that, when using f/16 on a sunny day, you can use a shutter speed that is roughly equal to the ISO setting to achieve a proper exposure. For simplification purposes, we will use an ISO of 100.

RECIPROCAL EXPOSURES: ISO 100

F-STOP	2.8	4	5.6	8	11	16	22
SHUTTER SPEED	1/4000	1/2000	1/1000	1/500	1/250	1/125	1/60

If you were to use any one of these combinations, they would each have the same result in terms of the exposure (how much light hits the camera's sensor) but would produce very different depths of field. Also take note that every time we cut the f-stop in half, we reciprocated by doubling our shutter speed. For those of you wondering why f/5.6 is half of f/8, it's because those numbers are actually fractions based on the opening of the lens in relation to its focal length. This means that a lot of math goes into merely figuring out what the total area of a lens opening is, so you just have to take it on faith that f/5.6 is half of f/8 but twice as much as f/4. A good way to remember which opening is larger is to think of your camera lens as a pipe that controls the flow of water. If you had a pipe that was 1/2 inch in diameter (f/2) and one that was 1/8 inch (f/8), which would allow more water to flow through? It would be the 1/2-inch pipe. The same idea works here with f-stops; f/2 is a larger opening than f/4 or f/8 or f/16.

RECIPROCAL EXPOSURES: ISO 200

F-STOP	2.8	4	5.6	8	11	16	22
SHUTTER SPEED	1/8000	1/4000	1/2000	1/1000	1/500	1/250	1/125

Now that we know this, we can start using this information to make intelligent choices in terms of shutter speeds and f-stops. Let's bring the third element into this by changing our ISO by one stop, from 100 to 200.

Notice that since we doubled the sensitivity of the sensor, we now require half as much exposure as before.

Let's use the exposure setting of f/16 at 1/250 of a second for a sunny day for purposes of our graph. Why bother with all of these reciprocal values when this one setting will give us a properly exposed image? The answer is that the f-stop and shutter speed also control two other important aspects of our image: motion and depth of field.

MOTION AND DEPTH OF FIELD

There are distinct characteristics related to changes in aperture and shutter speed. Shutter speed controls the length of time the light has to strike the sensor; consequently, it also controls the blurriness (or lack of blurriness) of the image. The less time light has to hit the sensor, the less time your subjects have to move around and become blurry. This lets you control things like freezing the motion of a fast-moving subject or intentionally blurring subjects to give the feel of energy and motion (**Figure 2.8**).

ISO 640
1/40 sec.
f/2.8
35mm lens

FIGURE 2.8
A slower shutter will convey motion when you are photographing moving objects. How much motion you show will depend on the shutter speed used. Here I wanted the image of the train to be very blurred, so I used a very slow shutter speed. If I had wanted to freeze motion I would have used a faster shutter speed.

The aperture controls the amount of light that comes through the lens, but also determines which areas of the image will be in focus. This is referred to as depth of field, and it is an extremely valuable creative tool. The smaller the opening (the larger the number, such as f/22), the greater the sharpness of objects from near to far. A large opening (or small number, like f/2.8) means more blurring of objects that are not at the same distance as the subject you are focusing on (**Figure 2.9**).

As we further explore the features of the camera, we will learn not only how to use the elements of exposure to capture properly exposed photographs, but also how we can make adjustments to emphasize our subject. It is the manipulation of these elements—motion and focus—that will take your images to the next level.

ISO 400
1/100 sec.
f/5.6
33mm lens

FIGURE 2.9
Isolating a subject is accomplished by using a large aperture, which produces a narrow area of sharp focus. Here I was able to isolate Tensing's pads by using the largest available aperture.

Chapter 2 Assignments

Formatting your card

Even if you have already begun using your camera, make sure you are familiar with formatting the Secure Digital card. If you haven't done so already, follow the directions given earlier in the chapter and format as described (make sure you save any images that you may have already taken). Then perform the format function every time you have downloaded or saved your images, or use a new card.

Checking your firmware version

Using the most up-to-date version of the camera firmware will ensure that your camera is functioning properly. Use the menu to find your current firmware version and then update as necessary using the steps listed in this chapter.

Cleaning your sensor

You probably noticed the sensor-cleaning message the first time you turned your camera on. Make sure to adjust the frequency of sensor cleaning to what works for you. Try setting it to Clean on Startup/Shutdown so that you don't have to remember to clean every time you change your lens.

Exploring your image formats

I want you to become familiar with all of the camera features before using the RAW format, but take a little time to explore the format menu so you can see what options are available to you.

Exploring your lens

If you are using a zoom lens, spend a little time shooting with all of the different focal lengths, from the widest to the longest. See just how much of an angle you can cover with your widest lens setting. How much magnification will you be able to get from the telephoto setting? Try shooting the same subject with a variety of focal lengths to note the differences in how the subject looks, and also the relationship between the subject and the other elements in the photo.

Share your results with the book's Flickr group!
Join the group here: flickr.com/groups/nikond7100_fromsnapshotstogreatshots.

3

ISO 100
20 sec.
f/20
27mm lens

The Auto Modes

GETTING STARTED WITH THE SCENE/SPECIAL EFFECTS MODES

Every digital photographer I know has taken photographs using what I call the green zone, or auto zone, and I'm not ashamed to admit that I still hang out there from time to time. The Nikon D7100 has done an incredible job of simplifying some of the most complex camera settings and creating an excellent baseline for many shots. In this chapter we're going to focus on how to use the built-in scene modes and the advantages even some of the more experienced photographers can gain from using these presets. Next we will discuss some of the fun uses as well as the limitations of the special effects modes. Let's take a look at these different modes and how and when to use them.

PORING OVER THE PICTURE

California's State Route 1 is hands-down my favorite scenic drive in all of North America. The highway stretches along some of the most breathtaking coastline in California. It's a strong reminder that capturing a great landscape doesn't always require one to travel too far off the beaten path. Often, what's more important is being prepared and being willing to take advantages of the many scenic turnouts along your journey. Keeping your tripod in the car and a camera nearby is half the battle in capturing great memories; the other half is simply making time!

The long exposure was necessary in creating the smooth, misty effect from waves.

ISO 100
23 sec.
f/20
16mm lens

Using a neutral density filter coupled with a low ISO and a high f-stop allowed me to create a longer exposure.

The Landscape scene mode increased the saturation of blue and green in the image.

A lower ISO helped maintain high image quality, with very little digital noise.

AUTO MODE

Auto mode is all about thought-free photography (**Figure 3.1**). There is little to nothing for you to do in this mode except point and shoot. Your biggest concern when using Auto mode is focusing. The camera will use the automatic focusing modes to achieve the best possible focus for your picture. Naturally, the camera is going to assume that the object that is closest to the camera is the one that you want to have the sharpest focus. Simply press the shutter button down halfway while looking through the viewfinder and you should see one of the focus points light up over the subject. Of course, you know that putting your subject in the middle of the picture is not usually the best way to compose your shot. So wait for the chirp to confirm that the focus has been set, and then, while still holding down the button, recompose your shot. Now just press down the shutter button the rest of the way to take the photo. It's that easy (**Figure 3.2**). The camera will take care of all your exposure decisions, including when to use flash.

FIGURE 3.1

To shoot in Auto mode, all you need to do is press the Mode dial lock release and turn the Mode dial so the green camera icon lines up with the white line. It's as simple as that!

FIGURE 3.2
Auto mode works great a large percentage of the time, so don't hesitate to use it. This photograph was taken while I was fly-fishing on the Deschutes River in Oregon. I had little time to think about my settings, so I put the camera on green, or Auto mode, and captured a cute moment.

ISO 400
1/250 sec.
f/5.6
300mm lens

I always tell my workshop students, if you're not sure of what setting to use, or if exposure, aperture, and speed are confusing, then start by using Auto mode. This mode can be an excellent learning tool. Take a photograph using Auto mode and note the ISO, aperture, and speed the camera uses. This is a great way to become familiar with settings. Then, as you become more familiar with them, you can begin to change them to better create your vision.

FLASH OFF MODE

 Sometimes you will be in a situation where the light levels are low but you don't want to use the flash. It could be that you are shooting in a place that restricts flash photography, such as your child's play or a museum, or maybe you want to take advantage of the available light, as when shooting candles on a birthday cake. This is where Flash Off mode comes into play (**Figure 3.3**).

By keeping the flash from firing, you will be able to use just the available ambient light while the camera automatically modi-

FIGURE 3.3
To shoot in Flash off mode, press the Mode dial lock release and turn the Mode dial to the Flash Off symbol. This will prevent your flash from firing.

fies the ISO setting to assist you in getting a good exposure (**Figure 3.4**). If the camera estimates that the shutter speed is going to be slow enough to introduce camera shake, it will list the shutter speed as "Lo" so that you know to check the camera settings. Fortunately, most of the new Vibration Reduction (VR) lenses being sold today allow you to hand-hold the camera at much slower shutter speeds and still get great results. The two downfalls to this mode are the Auto ISO setting, which will quickly take your ISO setting up as high as 25600, and the possibility of getting blur from subject movement.

FIGURE 3.4
Flash would have
ruined this shot of
an Indian woman at
a festival in North-
ern India. The flame
was lighting her
face beautifully, and
the flash would have
created a harsh,
unwanted light.

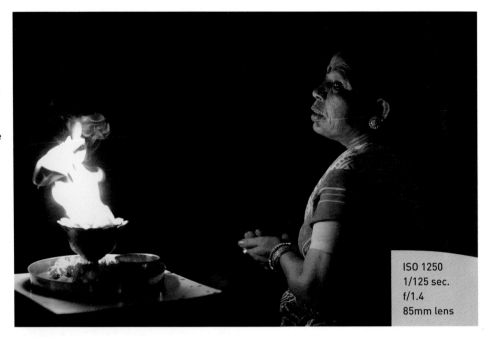

ISO 1250
1/125 sec.
f/1.4
85mm lens

SCENE MODES

 Most digital SLR cameras will have only about 7 or 8 automatic modes at their disposal, but the D7100 takes things to a whole new level with 16 additional scene modes to choose from (**Figure 3.5**). Nikon has anticipated many of the typical shooting scenarios that you will encounter and created scene modes that are optimized for those situations. We're going to focus on a few of the most popular modes in detail, but first, here's how to find them.

FIGURE 3.5
Remember, you have 16 scene modes to choose from, so have fun and experiment a little.

1. Set the Mode dial to the Scene setting.

2. Press the *i* or Info button to turn on the information screen on the back of the camera.

3. Rotate the main Command dial until the appropriate scene appears on the information screen.

PORTRAIT MODE

As mentioned before, Auto mode is accurate much of the time, but one of the problems with Full Auto mode is that it has no idea what type of subject you are photographing and, therefore, has no idea what depth of field to use. Shooting portraits is a perfect example. Typically, when you are taking a photograph of someone, you want the emphasis of the picture to be on the person, not necessarily the stuff going on in the background.

FIGURE 3.6
Portrait scene mode creates soft and natural-looking skin tones.

This is what Portrait mode is all about (**Figure 3.6**). When you set your camera to this mode, you are telling the camera to select a larger aperture (lower f-stop number) so that the depth of field is much narrower and will make objects in the background blurrier. This blurry background places the attention on your subject (**Figure 3.7**). The other feature of this mode is the automatic selection of the D7100's built-in Portrait picture control (we'll go into more detail about picture controls in later chapters). This feature is optimized for skin tones and will also be a little softer, to improve the look of skin.

USING THE BEST LENS FOR GREAT PORTRAITS

When using Portrait mode, use a lens length that is 50mm or longer. The longer lens will give you a natural view of the subject, as well as aid in keeping the depth of field narrow.

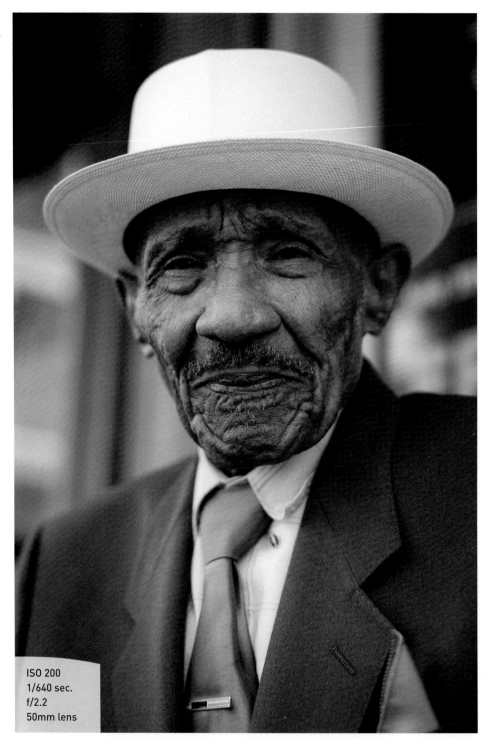

FIGURE 3.7
Portrait mode helps isolate your subject from the background, making the subject the main focus of the image.

ISO 200
1/640 sec.
f/2.2
50mm lens

LANDSCAPE MODE

As you might have guessed, Landscape mode has been optimized for shooting landscape images (**Figure 3.8**). Particular emphasis is placed on the picture control, with the camera trying to boost the greens and blues in the image (**Figure 3.9**). This makes sense, because the typical landscape would be outdoors, where grass, trees, and skies should look more colorful. This picture control also boosts the sharpness that is applied during processing. The camera uses the lowest ISO settings possible in order to keep digital noise to a minimum.

FIGURE 3.8
Landscape scene mode will increase color saturation and turn off the built-in flash and AF-assist illuminator.

The downfall to this setting is that, once again, there is little control over the camera settings. The focus mode can be changed—but only from AF-A to Manual. This means that either the camera will decide what to focus on for you, or you will need to use the manual focus feature in order to override the auto focus. Other changeable functions include Image Quality, ISO, and AF-area mode. Note that the flash cannot be used while you are in Landscape mode.

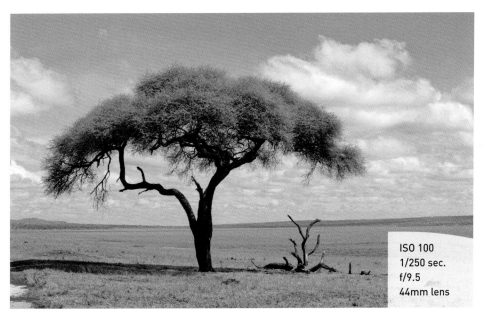

FIGURE 3.9
A low ISO helped to keep digital noise to a minimum, while the blue skies and red mud benefited by the increased saturation.

ISO 100
1/250 sec.
f/9.5
44mm lens

CLOSE UP MODE

Although most zoom lenses don't support true "macro" settings, that doesn't mean you can't shoot some great close-up photos. The key is to use your camera-to-subject distance to fill the frame while still being able to achieve sharp focus. This means that you move yourself as close as possible to your subject while still being able to get a good sharp focus. Often, your lens will be marked with the minimum focusing distance. On the 18–105mm zoom, it is about 8 inches with the lens set to 75mm. To help get the best focus in the picture, Close Up mode will use

FIGURE 3.10
Close Up scene mode is best used for flowers, small objects, and insects. If you're into macro photography, then this is the mode to use.

the smallest aperture it can while keeping the shutter speed fast enough to get a sharp shot (**Figures 3.10** and **3.11**). It does this by raising the ISO or turning on the built-in flash—or a combination of the two.

Fortunately, there are several other settings that you can change in this mode. The flash will be set to Auto by default, but you can also change it to Auto-redeye and Off, depending on your need. The ISO can be changed from the Auto setting to one of your own choosing. This probably needs to be done only in low-light settings when Auto ISO starts to move up to maintain exposure values. Other settings that can be changed are Image Quality, Release mode, Focus mode (AF-A or Manual), and AF-area mode.

FIGURE 3.11
Close Up mode provided the proper exposure to capture the smallest of details.

ISO 200
1/320 sec.
f/5.6
75mm lens

SPORTS MODE

While this is called Sports mode, you can use it for any moving subject that you are photographing (**Figure 3.12**). The mode is built on the principles of sports photography: continuous focusing, large apertures, and fast shutter speeds (**Figure 3.13**). To handle these requirements, the camera sets the focus mode to Dynamic, the aperture to a very large opening, and the ISO to Auto. Overall, these are sound settings that will capture most moving subjects well. We will take an in-depth look at all of these features, like Continuous Drive mode, in Chapter 5.

FIGURE 3.12
Sports mode scene is best used for when you want to freeze motion. When you're using this mode, the built-in flash and AF-assist illuminator will be turned off.

You can, however, run the risk of too much digital noise in your picture if the camera decides that you need a very high ISO (such as 3200). This is why you have the ability to change some options within Sports mode, such as ISO and Release mode (single and continuous). Also, when using Sports mode, you can change the focus mode from AF-A to Manual. This is especially handy if you know when and where the action will take place and want to prefocus the camera on a spot and wait for the right moment to take the photo.

FIGURE 3.13
This is the type of shot that was made for Sports mode, where action-freezing shutter speeds and continuous focusing work in harmony to capture the moment.

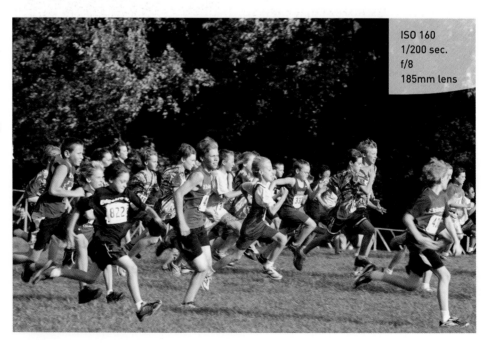

ISO 160
1/200 sec.
f/8
185mm lens

ISO 100
.6 sec.
f/22
80mm lens

SUNSET MODE

Here's a dirty secret—every photographer I know, whether professional or amateur, has taken his or her fair share of sunset photos. Sunset mode is a great way to capture a beautiful scene at dusk. What I love about this setting is that most sunsets are fairly predictable, so the automatic mode works great (**Figure 3.14**). This setting will increase the saturation and optimize the colors present in a sunset. If you're on vacation or just want to enjoy the moment, the last thing you need to worry about is fumbling

FIGURE 3.15
The key to taking great sunset photos is being patient. It's better to be early than late and stick with the shot until the sun goes all the way down. Often the reflection of the sunset can be as beautiful as the sunset itself.

FIGURE 3.14
Sunset scene mode creates deeper hues during sunset and sunrise. A tripod is recommended with this mode.

around with camera settings. Just move the dial to Sunset mode, sit back, relax, and let your camera do the work (**Figure 3.15**). One word of advice—this mode uses a longer exposure, so to avoid blurry photos try to use a tripod or steady your camera on a solid, level surface. You do have the option to change your ISO in this mode. If you're unable to steady your camera on a tripod or solid surface, I recommend increasing your ISO so that your speed is equal to or greater than the focal length of your lens. By doing this, you reduce your chances of camera shake (blurry photos).

CHILD MODE

FIGURE 3.17
Child mode tries to use a fast shutter speed, as well as making colors more vibrant. I didn't have a lot of time to capture this shot before she was going to pull off her mustache. I'm so glad that I was able to get the shot of my good friend John and his granddaughter.

Photographing children can be tough. Those little stinkers are fast, and if you've ever tried to photograph a two-year-old, you know the challenge of getting him or her to sit still. Child mode tries to solve this problem by blending the Sports and Portrait modes (**Figures 3.16** and **3.17**). Understanding that children are seldom still, the camera will try to use a slightly faster shutter speed to freeze any movement. The picture control feature has also been optimized to render bright, vivid colors that one normally associates with pictures of children. It's a great mode to use for kids on the go, or to capture a very brief moment that you don't want to miss.

FIGURE 3.16
Child scene mode is best used for snapshots of children on the go.

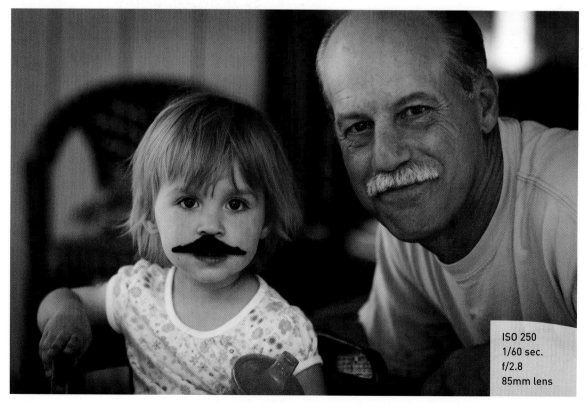

ISO 250
1/60 sec.
f/2.8
85mm lens

DUSK/DAWN

Some great photo opportunities take place before the sun rises and after it sets. The only problem is that the typical camera settings don't truly capture the vibrancy of the colors. The Dusk/Dawn camera setting is optimized for low-light photography and helps boost colors and eliminate noise from longer exposures. This mode is very similar to Sunset, but it uses a cooler white balance (**Figure 3.18**).

FIGURE 3.18
The Dusk/Dawn scene mode maintains the muted colors of early morning and evening. The flash and AF-assist illuminator turn off in this mode. A tripod is recommended due to potentially longer shutter speeds.

NIGHT PORTRAIT

Use this setting to help expose the background of your subject. For instance, if I'm taking a night portrait of a friend in front of Christmas lights, then I would use this setting. It tells your camera to use a slower than normal shutter speed so that the background has more time to be properly exposed (**Figure 3.19**).

FIGURE 3.19
The Night Portrait scene mode helps balance the subject and the background in low light. A tripod is recommended for low-light situations.

BEACH/SNOW

Shooting in a bright environment like the beach or a ski resort can have a bad effect on your images. The problem is that beaches and snow often reflect a lot of light and can fool the camera's light meter into underexposing. To solve this problem, you can use the Beach/Snow scene mode (**Figure 3.20**), which will overexpose slightly, giving you a much more accurate exposure.

FIGURE 3.20
The Beach/Snow scene mode helps you capture vacations by the water or in winter, when the brightness of the sand or snow could otherwise trick the camera into underexposing. The built-in flash and AF-assist illuminator are turned off in this mode.

PARTY/INDOOR

This mode is very much like the Night Portrait mode, except it is optimized for indoor use (**Figure 3.21**). The flash is automatically set to Auto-redeye and will use the redeye reduction lamp to help eliminate the redeye problem that often occurs when using the flash indoors.

NIGHT LANDSCAPE

A tripod or stable shooting surface is definitely recommended for Night Landscape mode (**Figure 3.22**). By using low ISOs, longer shutter speeds, and noise reduction, you can capture great cityscapes, with more accurate colors. The flash and focus-assist functions are turned off for this mode, so focusing might be a little difficult. If so, try moving your focus point to a different location.

FOOD

Food photography is very popular of late, and Nikon has provided you with a scene mode that is perfect for this type of work (**Figure 3.23**). When you select this mode, the camera will use large apertures for fairly narrow depth of field, slightly overexposed settings to keep things bright, and a picture control that makes colors slightly more vivid.

FIGURE 3.21
The Party/Indoor scene mode is great for birthday parties or weddings when you want to capture a special moment.

FIGURE 3.22
The Night Landscape scene mode helps reduce noise and unnatural colors. This mode is great for capturing a city skyline at night. A tripod is recommended so that the lights don't get blurred with a slow shutter speed.

FIGURE 3.23
The Food scene mode creates vivid colors. A tripod is advised with this mode; you will have use of the flash if needed.

AUTUMN COLORS

If you live in an area that has great fall color (like I do), you will want to give this mode a try (**Figure 3.24**). The big advantage to this scene mode is that it is optimized for the red and yellow hues that are present in autumn, and it really makes them pop. It also turns off the flash, because the light from a flash can wash out the color in the leaves. Try using this mode when the leaves have turned and the skies are overcast. You will get some amazing color in your images.

FIGURE 3.24
The Autumn Colors scene mode creates bright yellows and reds in autumn leaves. A tripod is recommended; flash is unavailable in this mode.

BLOSSOM

This mode is very similar to the Landscape setting but with a few slight adjustments. The color settings for Blossom have been optimized for use outdoors where there are many flowers in full bloom (**Figure 3.25**).

FIGURE 3.25
The Blossom scene mode is best used when you are photographing a field of flowers. A tripod is recommended to avoid blur, and flash will be unavailable.

CANDLELIGHT

Sometimes it's pretty easy to know when to use a particular mode. This mode is similar to the Flash Off mode, but it is tweaked for the color of candlelight and will give you much more pleasing results (**Figure 3.26**). If you are photographing people in candlelight, try using a tripod and have them hold fairly still to reduce image blur.

FIGURE 3.26
The Candlelight scene mode helps in low-light conditions. The built-in flash is disabled, and a tripod is recommended.

PET PORTRAIT

This mode is similar to the Portrait mode in that it uses larger apertures and faster shutter speeds (**Figure 3.27**). The difference is that Portrait mode is optimized for human skin, with adjustments to the hues and color values. Pets don't normally have much, if any, skin showing, so the sharpness and hues are adjusted accordingly.

FIGURE 3.27

The Pet Portrait scene mode works well when you're photographing a pet and don't want to scare it off with the AF-assist illuminator.

SPECIAL EFFECTS

 The D7100 takes scene modes to the next level by offering seven different special effects that can be used for creating still images or movies. Honestly, many special effects (**Figure 3.28**) features seem a bit hokey to me, but they may come in handy when trying to create unique effects for videos, or if you're just in the mood to have a little fun.

FIGURE 3.28

To activate the Effects mode press the Mode dial release and turn the Mode dial to Effects while rotating the main Command dial to your desired effect.

NIGHT VISION

This effects mode comes in handy when you're trying to capture monochrome images at a high ISO. Many times you'll need to use manual focus because auto-focus will not be able to determine the focus point due to the low-light conditions. A tripod is highly recommended to avoid camera shake (**Figure 3.29**).

FIGURE 3.29

It's best to turn off AF-assist illuminator (custom settings a7) when shooting landscapes.

COLOR SKETCH

The camera renders a color sketch of the framed subject. You can use this mode to create a cartoonlike effect in your still images or, in movie mode, create series of images that will be played back in a slideshow fashion. Live view can be used during this mode, but autofocus will not be available when capturing the images (**Figure 3.30**).

FIGURE 3.30
Use the Color Sketch effect to create a cartoon or series of images to create a flipbook effect.

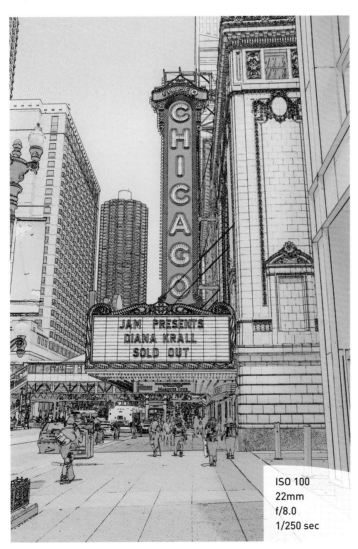

ISO 100
22mm
f/8.0
1/250 sec

MINIATURE EFFECT

Out of all the effects, this will probably be the most popular among photographers, because it gives the illusion of greater depth of field control via selective focus. The ability to make subjects in the distance appear as miniature is very much in vogue right now, in conjunction with time-lapse photography (**Figure 3.31**).

To alter the focus plane:

1. Press the LV button.

2. Press OK on the Multi-selector to activate the yellow depth of field lines. Next, use the Multi-selector's arrows to rotate and increase or decrease blur effect.

3. Press OK to return to LV to continue shooting with your new depth of field parameters.

FIGURE 3.31

Use this effect to create a unique and selective focus. Sound is disabled when using this mode for movies.

SELECTIVE COLOR

Use this effect to create black-and-white images with selective color turned on. Honestly, I've found this function to be a bit cumbersome and ineffective. If you're serious about using selective color with your black-and-white work, then I strongly urge you to consider Silver Efex Pro 2 (the industry standard in black-and-white conversion). Refer to page 182 of your manual to learn how to select colors in your image (**Figure 3.32**).

FIGURE 3.32

Use the Selective Color effect to create a black-and-white image with select areas of color.

SILHOUETTE

Using the Silhouette mode (**Figure** 3.33) does things like adjust the exposure for the brightest area of the scene as well as turn off the D-Lighting feature (see Chapter 11 for more on D-Lighting). This is necessary, because D-Lighting tries to boost exposure in shadow areas, which is the opposite of what you want when trying to get a nice silhouette.

FIGURE 3.33
The Silhouette effect creates a silhouette of the subject against brighter backgrounds. A tripod is recommended for this mode.

HIGH KEY

If Low Key mode means dark, then it's probably pretty easy to guess what High Key is for (**Figure** 3.34). Images that are bright throughout can present a different sort of challenge, with the bright environment tending to fool the camera into making an image that is darker than desired. Using the High Key setting forces the camera to over-expose a little and really lighten up those bright objects in your image.

FIGURE 3.34
The High Key effect creates very light and bright images; as with the Low Key mode, the flash is turned off.

LOW KEY

Low-key photos are typically meant to have an overall dark look. Much like in the beach or snow scenario only in reverse, your camera's light meter will usually try to add some exposure when shooting a low-key scene to make everything brighter. If you want to keep things on the dark side, use Low Key mode (**Figure** 3.35), which will keep the flash turned off and underexpose elements just a little bit.

FIGURE 3.35
The Low Key effect is best for times when you want to create a dark or subdued image. It will turn off the flash and is best used with a tripod.

WHEN YOU MAY NOT WANT TO USE AUTO MODE

With so many easy-to-use camera modes, why would anyone ever want to use anything else? Well, the first thing that comes to my mind is control. It is the number one benefit of using a digital SLR camera. The ability to control every aspect of your photography will open up creative avenues that just aren't always available in the automatic scene or effects modes. Let's face it: There is a reason that the Mode dial is split into two different categories. Let's look at what we are giving up when we work in the scene or effects modes.

- **White balance.** There is no choice available for white balance. You are simply stuck with the Auto setting. This isn't necessarily a bad thing, but your camera doesn't always get it right. And in the scene modes there is just no way to change it.

- **Picture control.** All of the automatic modes have specifically tuned picture controls. Some of them use the control presets such as Landscape or Vivid, but there is no way to change the characteristics of the controls while in the auto modes.

- **Metering.** All of the auto scene modes use the Matrix Metering mode to establish the proper exposure. This is generally not a downside, but specific scenarios would benefit from a center- or spot-metering solution, which we will cover in later chapters.

- **Exposure Compensation.** You will notice that in each and every automatic scene and effects mode, the ability to adjust the exposure through the use of the Exposure Compensation feature has been completely turned off. This makes it very difficult to make the slight exposure adjustments that are often needed.

- **Active D-Lighting.** This is another feature that is unavailable for changing in all of the auto modes. There are default settings for this feature that change from scene to scene, but there is no way for you to override the effect.

LIVE VIEW

Live View is the feature on your D7100 that allows you to see a real-time view of what the camera is looking at via the rear LCD. Using Live View can be extremely helpful in fine-tuning your focus while using a tripod or if you need to shoot from an angle that doesn't let you put your eye up to the viewfinder. It is also an excellent way of previewing any changes to white balance or the picture style, because their effects will be visible on the screen. You'll find more on Live View in Chapters 6 and 7.

- **Flash Compensation.** Just as with Exposure Compensation, there is no way to make any adjustments to the power output of the flash. This means that you are stuck with whatever the camera feels is correct, even if it is too weak or too strong for your particular subject.

- **Exposure bracketing.** One way to make sure that you have at least one good exposure is to use the bracketing feature of the camera, which takes images at varying exposures so you can get just the right look for your image. Unfortunately, this feature is also unavailable when using the scene and effects modes.

Another thing you will find when using any of the automatic modes is that there are fewer choices in the camera menus for you to adjust. Each scene or effects mode presents its own set of restrictions for the available menu items. These aren't the only restrictions to using the automatic scene and effects modes, but they should be enough to make you want to explore the other side of the Mode dial, which I like to call the professional modes.

FOCUS MODES ON THE NIKON D7100

Three focus modes are available on the D7100. Depending on the type of photography you are doing, you can easily select the mode that will be most beneficial. The standard mode is called AF-S, which allows you to focus on one spot and hold that focus until you take the picture or release the shutter button. The AF-C mode will constantly refocus the camera on your subject the entire time you are depressing the shutter release button. This is great for sports and action photography. The AF-A mode is a combination of both of the previous modes; it uses AF-S mode unless it senses that the subject is moving, when it will switch to AF-C mode.

Chapter 3 Assignments

These assignments will have you shooting in the various automatic scene and effects modes so that you can experience the advantages and disadvantages of using them in your daily photography.

Shooting in Auto mode

It's time to give up complete control and just concentrate on what you see in the viewfinder. Set your camera to Auto and practice shooting in a variety of conditions, both indoors and outside. Take notice of the camera settings when you are reviewing your pictures. Try using the AF-S focus point to pick a spot to focus on and then recompose before taking the picture.

Checking out Portrait mode

Grab your favorite photogenic person and start shooting in Portrait mode. Try switching between Auto and Portrait modes while photographing the same person in the same setting. You should see a difference in the sharpness of the background as well as the skin tones. If you are using a zoom lens, set it to about 50mm, if available.

Capturing the scenery with Landscape and Close Up modes

Take your camera outside for some landscape and macro work. First, find a nice scene and then, with your widest available lens, take some pictures using Landscape mode. Then switch back to Auto so that you can compare the settings used for each image as well as the changes to colors and sharpness. Now, while you are still outside, find something in the foreground—a leaf or a flower—and switch the camera to Close Up mode. See how close you can get, and take note of the f-stop that the mode uses. Then switch to Auto and shoot the same subject.

Stopping the action with Sports mode

This assignment will require that you find a subject that is in motion. That could be the traffic in front of your home or your child at play. The only real requirement is that the subject be moving. This will be your opportunity to test out Sports mode. There isn't a lot to worry about here. Just point and shoot. Try shooting a few frames one at a time and then go ahead and hold down the shutter button and shoot a burst of about five or six frames. It will help if your subject is in good available light to start with so that the camera won't be forced to use high ISOs.

Let your camera do the mentoring

How many times have you wondered what settings you should use for a particular shot? Here's what I tell my students—if you're in doubt, place your camera on the auto settings and take note of what your camera thinks is the best ISO, aperture, and speed. Your camera won't always be right, but it's going to give you a great baseline. Then adjust one element at a time and retake the shot to see what happens. This will help you understand how each of the settings affects the shot.

Share your results with the book's Flickr group!
Join the group here: flickr.com/groups/nikond7100_fromsnapshotstogreatshots.

4

ISO 100
1/125 sec.
f/9
35mm lens

The Professional Modes

TAKING YOUR PHOTOGRAPHY TO THE NEXT LEVEL

If you talk to professional photographers, you will find that the majority of them use a few selective modes that offer the greatest amount of control over their photography. To anyone who has been involved with photography for any period of time, these modes are the backbones of the art. They allow you to influence two of the most important factors in taking great photographs: *aperture* and *shutter speed.* To access these modes, you simply turn the Mode dial to one of the letter-designated modes and begin shooting. But wouldn't it be nice to know exactly what those modes control and how to make them do our bidding? Well, if you really want to take that next step in controlling your photography, it is essential that you understand not only how to control these modes but why you are controlling them. So let's move that Mode dial to the first of our professional modes, or as I like to think of it, professional light: Programmed Auto mode.

Bulb mode was a must here, since I needed to create an exposure over 30 seconds long.

I used a low ISO with a tripod to guarantee a high-quality image free of camera shake.

The wide-angle lens allowed me to fill the frame while being close to the subject.

ISO 100
240 sec.
f/22
24mm lens

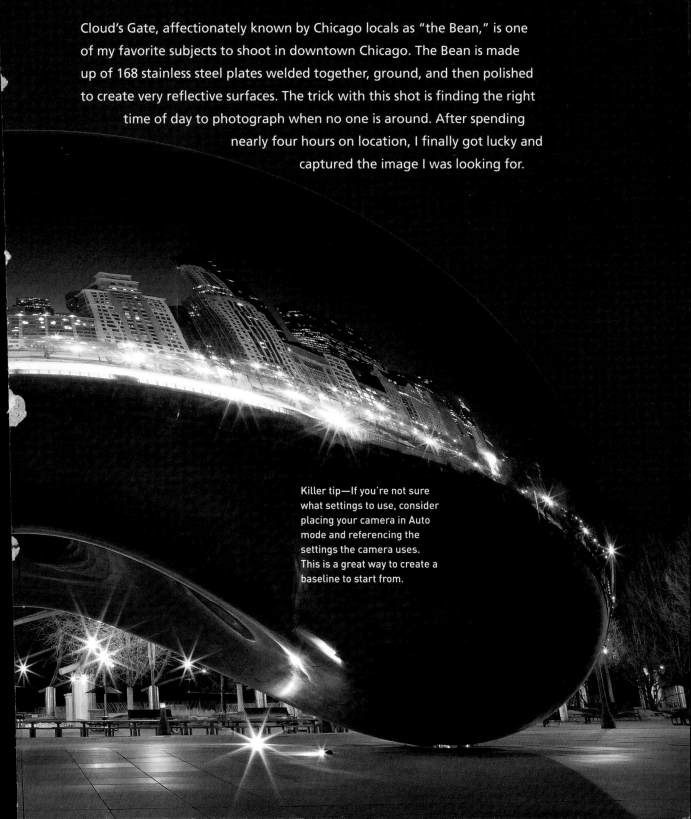

Cloud's Gate, affectionately known by Chicago locals as "the Bean," is one of my favorite subjects to shoot in downtown Chicago. The Bean is made up of 168 stainless steel plates welded together, ground, and then polished to create very reflective surfaces. The trick with this shot is finding the right time of day to photograph when no one is around. After spending nearly four hours on location, I finally got lucky and captured the image I was looking for.

Killer tip—If you're not sure what settings to use, consider placing your camera in Auto mode and referencing the settings the camera uses. This is a great way to create a baseline to start from.

P: PROGRAMMED AUTO MODE

 I call Programmed Auto mode, or P mode, "professional light" because it's a great mode to become familiar with as you transition from the automatic or scene modes (**Figure 4.1**) to Aperture Priority, Shutter Priority, or Manual mode. There is a reason that Programmed Auto mode is only one click away from the automatic modes: With respect to apertures and shutter speeds, the camera is doing most of the thinking for you. So if that is the case, why even bother with P mode?

FIGURE 4.1
Use Programmed Auto mode for flexible control and as a great place to start learning professional modes.

First, let me say that I rarely use Programmed Auto mode, because it just doesn't give as much control over the image-making process as the other professional modes. However, we all start somewhere, and much like many of you, I started fully automatic, moved to Programmed Auto mode, and now hang out in Aperture Priority most of the time. There are still occasions when Programmed Auto mode comes in handy, like when I am shooting in widely changing lighting conditions and I don't have the time to think through all of my options, or I'm not very concerned with having ultimate control of the scene. Think of a picnic outdoors in a partial shade and sun environment. I want great-looking pictures, but I'm not looking for anything to hang in a museum. If that's the scenario, why choose P mode over one of the scene modes? Because it gives me choices and control that none of the scene modes can deliver.

Manual Callout

To see available settings for each mode, check out the table on pages 47–54 of your owner's manual.

WHEN TO USE PROGRAMMED AUTO (P) MODE INSTEAD OF THE AUTOMATIC SCENE AND EFFECTS MODES

It's graduation time, and you're ready to move on to a more advanced mode but not quite ready to jump in with both feet. When does Programmed Auto mode come in handy?

- When shooting in a casual environment where quick adjustments are needed.

- When you want more control over the ISO.

- If you want to make corrections to the white balance.

- When you want to take advantage of the Flexible Program mode and change shutter speeds via aperture. Move the main Command dial to the left for small apertures to increase depth of field, or rotate the dial to the right for large apertures to create a shallow depth of field.

Let's go back to our picnic scenario. As I said, the light is moving from deep shadow to bright sunlight, which means that the camera is trying to balance our three photo factors (ISO, aperture, and shutter speed) to make a good exposure. From Chapter 1, we know that Auto ISO is generally not what we want except when shooting in Auto mode, so we have already turned that feature off (you did turn it off, didn't you?). Well, in P mode, you can choose which ISO you would like the camera to base its exposure on. The lower the ISO number, the better the quality of the photographs, but the less light sensitive the camera becomes. It's a balancing act, with the main goal always being to keep the ISO as low as possible—too low an ISO, and we will get camera shake in our images from a long shutter speed; too high an ISO, and we will have an unacceptable amount of digital noise (**Figures 4.2** and **4.3**). For now, let's go ahead and select ISO 400 so that we provide enough sensitivity for those shadows while allowing the camera to use shutter speeds that are fast enough to stop motion.

FIGURE 4.2
Look closely and you'll notice the image is grainy, or has small pixels. That's digital noise. Now, look at the same image taken at a lower 100 ISO.

FIGURE 4.3
Notice the detail in the black plastic and how little noise is in the image.

STARTING POINTS FOR ISO SELECTION

Many years ago camera manufacturers were racing to create cameras with more megapixels. Today the digital race is all about higher ISO. Photographers want to be able to shoot in lower light conditions without the risk of digital noise. There is a lot of discussion concerning ISO in this and other chapters, but it might be helpful if you know where your starting points should be for your ISO settings. The first thing you should always try to do is use the lowest possible ISO setting. Your D7100 has a working range of 100–6400. That being said, here are good starting points for your ISO settings:

- 100: Bright, sunny day

- 200: Hazy or outdoor shade on a sunny day

- 400: Indoor lighting at night or cloudy conditions outside

- 800: Late night, low-light conditions or sports arenas at night

- 1600: Very low light; possibly candlelight or events where no flash is allowed

- 3200–6400: Extreme low light (some digital noise will be present; however, less than ever before)

These are just suggestions; you'll have to adjust as necessary. Your ISO selection will depend on a number of factors that will be discussed later in the book.

With the ISO selected, we can now make use of the other controls built into Programmed Auto mode. By rotating the main Command dial, we now have the ability to shift the program settings. Remember, your camera is using the internal meter to pick what it deems suitable exposure values, but sometimes it doesn't know what it's looking at and how you want those values applied (**Figures 4.4** and **4.5**). With the program shift, you can influence what the shot will look like. Do you need faster shutter speeds in order to stop the action? Just turn the main Command dial to the right. Do you want a smaller aperture so that you get a narrow depth of field? Turn the dial to the left until you get the desired aperture. The camera shifts the shutter speed and aperture accordingly to get a proper exposure.

You will also notice that a small star will appear above the letter P in the viewfinder and the rear display if you rotate the main Command dial. This star is an indication that you modified the exposure from the one the camera chose. To go back to the default Programmed Auto exposure, simply turn the dial until the star goes away or switch to a different mode and then back to P mode again.

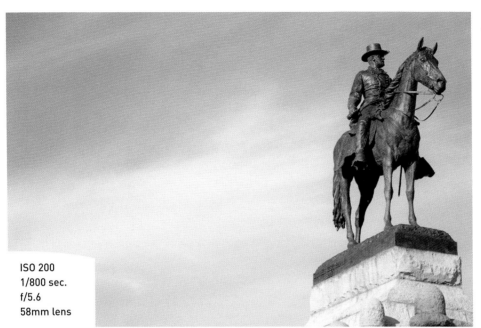

FIGURE 4.4
This image was shot using the Programmed Auto mode. In this image the shutter was faster because the image is lighter than Figure 4.5. Because the image is lighter, the camera needs less time to expose, so the shutter opens and closes very quickly—in this case, 1/160 of a second quicker.

ISO 200
1/800 sec.
f/5.6
58mm lens

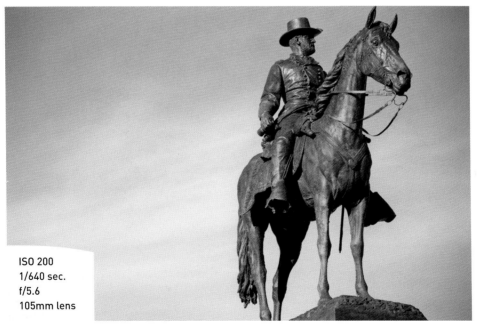

FIGURE 4.5
When we zoom in on the bronze statue, our image becomes darker than in Figure 4.4 because there is less of the bright blue sky. The camera needs more light to properly expose the image, so the shutter is left open longer.

ISO 200
1/640 sec.
f/5.6
105mm lens

Let's set up the camera for Programmed Auto mode and see how we can make all of this come together.

SETTING UP AND SHOOTING IN PROGRAMMED AUTO MODE

1. Turn your camera on and then turn the Mode dial to align the P with the indicator line.

2. Select your ISO by pressing and holding the ISO button on the back left of the camera while rotating the main Command dial with your thumb.

3. The ISO will appear on the top display. Choose your desired ISO, and release the ISO button on the left to lock in the change.

4. Point the camera at your subject and then activate the camera meter by depressing the shutter button halfway.

5. View the exposure information in the bottom area of the viewfinder or by looking at the top display panel.

6. While the meter is activated, use your thumb to roll the main Command dial left and right to see the changed exposure values.

7. Select the exposure that is right for you and start clicking. (Don't worry if you aren't sure what the right exposure is yet. We will work on making the right choices for those great shots beginning with the next chapter.)

S: SHUTTER PRIORITY MODE

 S mode is what we photographers commonly refer to as Shutter Priority mode. Just as the name implies, it is the mode that prioritizes or places major emphasis on the shutter speed above all other camera settings (**Figure 4.6**).

Just as with Programmed Auto mode, Shutter Priority mode gives us more freedom to control certain aspects of our photography. In this case, we are talking about shutter speed. The selected shutter

FIGURE 4.6
Shutter Priority mode is great for freezing or showing motion. Use this mode when your shutter speed is of utmost importance.

speed determines just how long you expose your camera's sensor to light. The longer it remains open, the more time your sensor has to gather light.

The shutter speed also, to a large degree, determines how sharp your photographs are. Even though an image may appear sharply in focus, any movement by the subject or the camera while the shutter is open can blur the image. If you think about it, when you are trying to show motion, you want a slower shutter speed because it blurs the image.

A good rule of thumb for avoiding blurry images is to always use a shutter speed as fast as your focal length. For instance, if I'm out photographing my daughter with an 80mm lens, then I'll want to make sure my shutter speed is at least 1/120 of a second, taking into account that the camera is not full frame, so the actual focal length is greater than the focal length of the lens. Anything less than that might cause camera shake (even if you're equipped with biceps as big as Popeye's). The D7100 has a 1.3x magnification, so if your focal length is 100mm, you shouldn't shoot less than 1/150 of a second.

SHUTTER SPEEDS

A *slow* shutter speed refers to leaving the shutter open for a long period of time—like 1/30 of a second or more. A *fast* shutter speed means that the shutter is open for a very short period of time—like 1/250 of a second or less. A faster shutter speed is used to stop motion, and a slower shutter speed is used to show motion.

WHEN TO USE SHUTTER PRIORITY (S) MODE

- When working with fast-moving subjects and you want to freeze the action (**Figure 4.7**); much more on this is in Chapter 5

- When you want to emphasize movement in your subject with motion blur (**Figure 4.8**)

- When you want to use a long exposure to gather light over a long period of time (**Figure 4.9**); more on this is in Chapter 8

- When you want to create that smooth-looking water in a waterfall or rapids in a creek or river (**Figure 4.10**)

FIGURE 4.7
Whenever I'm planning on freezing motion, I always make sure I'm shooting with a fast shutter speed. I knew the rodeo would be giving me lots of opportunities for that kind of action, so I set my speed to be very fast so that I could capture every movement of the horse and the rider.

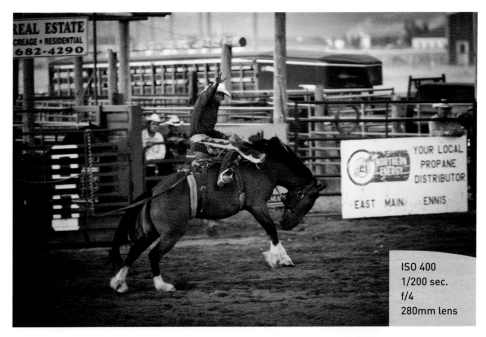

ISO 400
1/200 sec.
f/4
280mm lens

FIGURE 4.8
If you're photographing a fast-moving subject and wish to convey a sense of motion, always use a slower shutter. In this image I wanted to blur the background while freezing the subject, so it required me to use a slower shutter while following, or "panning," with the subject in focus.

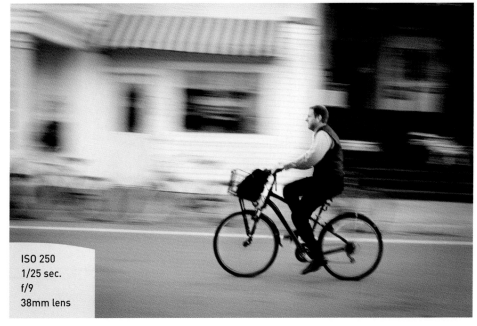

ISO 250
1/25 sec.
f/9
38mm lens

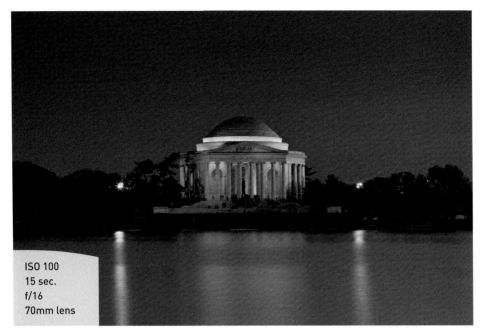

FIGURE 4.9
I took this very long exposure of the Jefferson Monument in Washington, DC, using a tripod and a cable release. There's no way I could have held the camera steady for 15 seconds! A tripod is a must for long exposures.

ISO 100
15 sec.
f/16
70mm lens

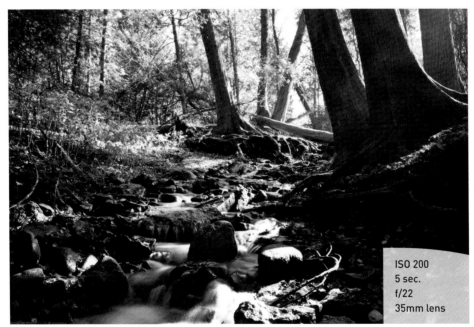

FIGURE 4.10
I used a cable release and tripod to photograph this small creek on Mackinac Island, Michigan. I was able to create a smooth look to the water by increasing the length of the exposure using Shutter Priority mode.

ISO 200
5 sec.
f/22
35mm lens

As you can see, the subject of your photo usually determines whether or not you will use Shutter Priority mode. It is important that you be able to previsualize the result of using a particular shutter speed. The great thing about shooting with digital cameras is that you get instant feedback by viewing your shot on the LCD. But what if your subject won't give you a do-over? Such is often the case when shooting sporting events. It's not like you can go ask your daughter to score another goal in her soccer game because your photograph was blurry from a slow shutter speed. This is why it's important to know what those speeds represent in terms of their capabilities to stop the action and deliver a blur-free shot.

First, let's examine just how much control you have over the shutter speeds. The D7100 has a shutter speed range from 1/8000 of a second all the way down to 30 seconds. With that much latitude, you should have enough control to capture almost any subject. The other thing to think about is that Shutter Priority mode is considered a semiautomatic mode. That means that you are taking control over one aspect of the total exposure while the camera handles the other. In this instance, you are controlling the shutter speed and the camera is controlling the aperture. This is important, because there will be times that you want to use a particular shutter speed but your lens won't be able to accommodate your request.

For example, you might encounter this problem when shooting in low-light situations: If you are shooting a fast-moving subject that will blur at a shutter speed slower than 1/125 of a second but your lens's largest aperture is f/3.5, you might find your aperture display in your viewfinder and the rear LCD panel will display the word "Lo." This is your warning that there won't be enough light available for the shot—due to the limitations of the lens—so your picture will be underexposed. Your only remedy is to increase your ISO to accommodate the shutter speed needed.

Another case where you might run into this situation is when you are shooting moving water. To get that look of smooth, flowing water, it's usually necessary to use a shutter speed at least as slow as 1/15 of a second. If your waterfall is in full sunlight, you may get a message that reads "Hi" because the lens you are using only stops down to f/22 at its smallest opening. In this instance, your camera is warning you that you will be overexposing your image. There are workarounds for these problems, which we will discuss later, but it is important to know that there can be limitations when using Shutter Priority mode.

1. Turn your camera on and then turn the Mode dial to align the S with the indicator line.

2. Select your ISO by pressing and holding the ISO button on the back left of the camera while rotating the main Command dial with your thumb.

3. The ISO will appear on the top display. Choose your desired ISO, and release the ISO button on the left to lock in the change.

4. Point the camera at your subject and then activate the camera meter by depressing the shutter button halfway.

5. View the exposure information in the bottom area of the viewfinder or by looking at the top display panel.

6. While the meter is activated, use your thumb to roll the main Command dial left and right to see the changed exposure values. Roll the dial to the right for faster shutter speeds and to the left for slower speeds.

A: APERTURE PRIORITY MODE

 Probably the mode most widely used by professional photographers, Aperture Priority is one of my personal favorites, and I believe that it will quickly become one of yours. Aperture Priority mode is also deemed a semiautomatic mode because it allows you to once again control one factor of exposure while the camera adjusts for the other (**Figure 4.11**).

Why is this one of my favorite modes? It's because the aperture of your lens dictates depth of field. Depth of field, along with

FIGURE 4.11
Use Aperture Priority mode when you need to control depth of field. This is my favorite shooting mode.

composition, is a major factor in how you direct attention to what matters in your image. It is the controlling factor of how much area in your image is sharp. If you want to isolate a subject from the background, such as when shooting a portrait, you can use a large aperture (low f-stop number) to keep the focus on your subject and make both the foreground and background blurry. If you want to keep the entire scene sharply focused, as with a landscape scene, then using a small aperture (high f-stop number) will render the greatest amount of depth of field possible.

WHEN TO USE APERTURE PRIORITY (A) MODE

- When shooting portraits or wildlife (**Figure 4.12**)

- When shooting most landscape photography (**Figure 4.13**)

- When shooting in bright skies consider silhouetting an image (**Figure 4.14**)

- When shooting cityscape photography, which often benefits from a large depth of field (**Figure 4.15**)

FIGURE 4.12
The lizard was very still so I was able to use a tripod and zoom in tight. The large aperture helped create a smooth, blurry background, also known as bokeh.

ISO 200
1/100 sec.
f/5
200mm lens

FIGURE 4.13
The smaller aperture setting brings sharpness to near and far objects.

ISO 200
1/200 sec.
f/10
27mm lens

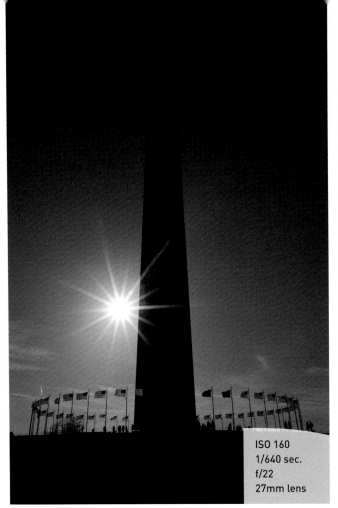

FIGURE 4.14
Using a very small aperture on a clear blue day, I was able to create this sunburst. Typically f/16 or higher will do the trick! Give it a try. The key ingredient is a clear sky, because clouds will diffuse the sun.

ISO 160
1/640 sec.
f/22
27mm lens

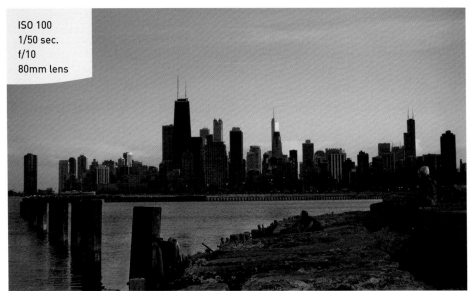

ISO 100
1/50 sec.
f/10
80mm lens

FIGURE 4.15
I wanted the foreground as well as the background in focus, so I used a wide-angle lens combined with a small aperture to maintain focus throughout the image. This is called a deep depth of field.

F-STOPS AND APERTURE

As discussed earlier, the numeric value of your lens aperture is described as an *f-stop*. The f-stop is one of those old photography terms that, technically, relates to the focal length of the lens (e.g., 200mm) divided by the effective aperture diameter. These measurements are defined as "stops" and work incrementally with your shutter speed to determine proper exposure. Older camera lenses used one-stop increments to assist in exposure adjustments, such as 1.4, 2, 2.8, 4, 5.6, 8, 11, 16, and 22. Each stop represents about half the amount of light entering the lens iris as the larger stop before it. Today, most lenses don't have f-stop markings, since all adjustments to this setting are performed via the camera's electronics. The stops are also now typically divided into 1/3-stop increments to allow much finer adjustments to exposures, as well as to match the incremental values of your camera's ISO settings, which are also adjusted in 1/3-stop increments.

I strongly recommend knowing your lens's aperture rating. Every lens has a marking on it with a number; f/1.4, f/2.8, or f/5.6 are all very common maximum aperture sizes. This number simply means the largest aperture your lens supports is f/1.4, f/2.8, or f/5.6, respectively. The D7100 kit ships with a standard 18–105mm lens with an f/3.5–f/5.6 variable maximum aperture **(Figure 4.16)**.

Knowing the limits of your lens aperture is crucial when using Aperture Priority. As a general rule, the lower the number on the lens, the "faster" it is (because it allows more light in to expose the image, thus reducing the amount of shutter time) and the sharper the image is. Typically, fast lenses are heavier and more expensive, but they're well worth the investment if you find yourself shooting in low-light conditions. The larger the aperture is, the better the exposure without having to increase ISO and introduce digital noise.

FIGURE 4.16
It's important to know the focal range and maximum aperture of your lens.

On the other hand, bright scenes require the use of a small aperture (such as f/16 or f/22), especially if you want to use a slower shutter speed. That small opening reduces the amount of incoming light, and this reduction of light requires that the shutter stay open longer.

ZOOM LENSES AND MAXIMUM APERTURES

Some zoom lenses (like the 18–105mm kit lens) have a variable maximum aperture. This means that the largest opening will change depending on the zoom setting. In the example of the 18–105mm zoom, the lens has a maximum aperture of f/3.5 at 18mm and only f/5.6 when the lens is zoomed out to 105mm.

SETTING UP AND SHOOTING IN APERTURE PRIORITY MODE

1. Turn your camera on and then turn the Mode dial to align the A with the indicator line.

2. Select your ISO by pressing and holding the ISO button on the back left of the camera while rotating the main Command dial with your thumb.

3. The ISO will appear on the top display. Choose your desired ISO, and release the ISO button on the left to lock in the change.

4. Point the camera at your subject and then activate the camera meter by depressing the shutter button halfway.

5. View the exposure information in the bottom area of the viewfinder or by looking at the top display panel.

6. While the meter is activated, use your finger to roll the Sub-command dial left and right to see the changed exposure values. Roll the dial to the right for a smaller aperture (higher f-stop number) and to the left for a larger aperture (lower f-stop number).

M: MANUAL MODE

Manual mode is all about control. Keep in mind, this mode was not designed for those of us who want to go on autopilot and shoot to our heart's content. It was designed to allow the photographer to take complete control of shutter speed and aperture (**Figure 4.17**). The camera doesn't do any of the work for you.

FIGURE 4.17
For ultimate control of shutter speed and aperture, use Manual mode.

When you have your camera set to Manual (M) mode, the camera meter will give you a reading of the scene you are photographing. It's your job, though, to set both the f-stop (aperture) and the shutter speed to achieve a correct exposure. If you need a faster shutter speed, you will have to make the reciprocal change to your f-stop. Using any other mode, such as Shutter Priority or Aperture Priority, would mean that you just have to worry about one of these changes, but Manual mode means you have to do it all yourself. This can be a little challenging at first, but after a while you will have a complete understanding of how each change affects your exposure, which will, in turn, improve the way that you use the other modes.

WHEN TO USE MANUAL (M) MODE

- When lighting and exposure get tricky (**Figure 4.18**). Shooting indoors through glass can be especially tricky. The wonderful thing about your D7100 is that it has an incredible ISO range with relatively low digital noise.

- When your environment is fooling your light meter and you need to maintain a certain exposure setting (**Figure 4.19**). Beaches and snow are always a challenge for light meters. Whenever I'm shooting something in snow I find myself switching over to Manual mode.

- When shooting silhouetted subjects, which requires overriding the camera's meter readings (**Figure 4.20**).

FIGURE 4.18
I took this image of apes at a zoo behind glass and wanted to avoid having my flash trigger because that would have left a nasty reflection. I decided to bump up my ISO and use a large aperture to get this shot.

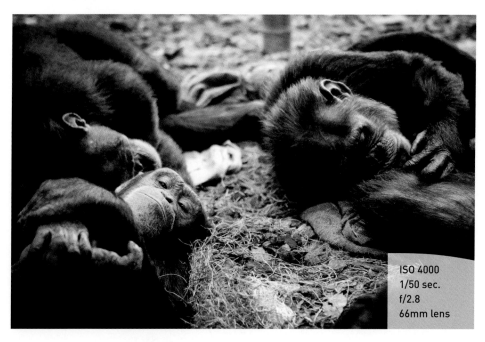

ISO 4000
1/50 sec.
f/2.8
66mm lens

FIGURE 4.19
A good rule of thumb in snow is to bump your exposure up one or two f-stops if it's really sunny. That should get you closer to the correct exposure.

ISO 200
1/400 sec.
f/11
85mm lens

ISO 100
1/3000 sec.
f/7.1
35mm lens

FIGURE 4.20
The camera's meter will do a great job most of the time, but when you want to get creative sometimes you need to use Manual mode. Using Manual mode allowed me to silhouette the buildings while maintaining the warm glow of the sun.

SETTING UP AND SHOOTING IN MANUAL MODE

1. Turn your camera on and then turn the Mode dial to align the M with the indicator line.

2. Select your ISO by pressing and holding the ISO button on the back left of the camera while rotating the main Command dial with your thumb.

3. The ISO will appear on the top display. Choose your desired ISO, and release the ISO button on the left to lock in the change.

4. Point the camera at your subject and then activate the camera meter by depressing the shutter button halfway.

5. View the exposure information in the bottom area of the viewfinder or by looking at the top display panel.

6. To set your exposure using shutter speed, while the meter is activated, use your thumb to roll the main Command dial left and right to change your shutter speed value until the exposure mark is lined up with the zero mark. The exposure information is displayed in the viewfinder using a scale with marks that run from –2 to +2 stops with 0 indicating proper exposure. As the indicator moves to the left, the image is being underexposed, or gets darker. Move the indicator to the right and the image is being overexposed, or gets brighter.

7. To set your exposure using the aperture, while the meter is activated, use your finger to roll the Sub-command dial left and right to see the changed exposure values. Roll the dial to the right for a smaller aperture (higher f-stop number) and to the left for a larger aperture (lower f-stop number).

8. Note: You might have good reasons to want to overexpose or underexpose an image. For instance, as a black-and-white photographer, I'll often overexpose my images by one-third of a stop to assure that my shadows have some details. This is just one of many creative reasons for adjusting your exposure differently than is suggested by the meter.

USER SETTINGS MODE—SAVING YOUR FAVORITE SETTINGS TO THE MODE DIAL

  User settings are a great feature if you're looking to have your favorite settings at the turn of a dial. These are located on the dial as U1 and U2. If you have a group of settings that you find you are using often and you want to have them close at hand, then these modes are handy for you.

- First, set the camera to your favorite settings, under any of the semiautomatic modes or Manual mode, adjusting aperture, shutter speed, ISO, flash, focus point, metering, and/or bracketing.

- Go to the setup menu, and click on Save User Settings (**A**), (**B**).

- Highlight U1 or U2, then click OK to save your settings (**C**).

- When you want to use those settings again, just rotate the top dial to U1 or U2, and the camera will choose your saved settings so that you're ready to go (**D**).

For more on setting up user modes, see page 55 of your owner's manual.

A

B

C

D

HOW I SHOOT: MY FAVORITE CAMERA SETTINGS

I'm generally a landscape and travel photographer, but like many of you, I enjoy photographing everything. There's very little that doesn't interest me. I have found throughout the years that I primarily use the Aperture Priority mode. Why? Often when I'm traveling and focusing on my street photography, I don't have time to worry about every single variable, and I've found focusing on aperture has given me the control I need for 95 percent of my photography. If I want an image to have a shallow depth of field, then I'll use a large aperture such as f/2.8, or if I'm shooting a landscape and I need a greater depth of field I'll use a smaller aperture such as f/16.

However, sometimes Aperture Priority just doesn't work. Maybe the lighting is tricky or it's close but not quite right. In those cases I'll switch over to Manual mode. Almost all of my landscape photography that I've shot during the golden hours was done in Manual mode because the light changes very quickly.

Each photographer has a different way of doing things. No one approach is necessarily better than the other. In the end, it's about creating your own system so that you're consistent. When you're consistent, you can measure results and then make changes accordingly.

When I first started out photographing in Aperture Priority, the biggest mistake I made was shooting with much too slow of a shutter speed. I would get blurry pictures and I would ask myself, "How did this happen? They looked super sharp when I took them." I would then look at the metadata (image information) and would see that I shot the blurry image at 1/30 of a second, way too slow for handholding a camera. So I learned my lesson and started shooting a little faster, and my results improved immensely.

Doing things consistently and measuring results is a great way to improve your photography. Don't ignore the metadata; it's very helpful in understanding why an image looks a certain way and learning how to change your setting the next time to make the image stronger.

While the other camera modes have their place, I think you will find that most professional photographers use the Aperture Priority and Shutter Priority modes for 90 percent of their shooting.

One big concern that I have when I am setting up my camera is just how low I can keep my ISO. This is always a priority for me, because a low ISO will deliver the cleanest image. I raise the ISO only as a last resort because each increase in sensitivity is an opportunity for more digital noise to enter my image.

To make quick changes while I shoot, I often use the Exposure Compensation feature (covered in Chapter 7) so that I can make small over- and underexposure changes. This is different than changing the aperture or shutter; it is more like fooling the camera meter into thinking the scene is brighter or darker than it actually is. To get to this function quickly, I simply press the Exposure Compensation button, right next to the shutter button, and then dial in the desired amount of compensation using the main Command dial. If you can't get the exact exposure you want with aperture and speed alone, make little adjustments to the exposure compensation.

One of the reasons some people change their exposure is to make corrections when there are "blinkies" in the rear LCD. Blinkies are the warning signal that part of the image has been overexposed to the point that there is no longer any detail in the highlights. When the Highlight Alert feature is turned on, the display will flash wherever the potential exists for overexposure. The black-and-white flashing will only appear in areas of your picture that are in danger of overexposure.

SETTING UP THE HIGHLIGHT ALERT FEATURE

1. Press the Menu button, and then use the Multi-selector to access the Playback menu.

2. Once in the Playback menu, move the Multi-selector to Playback Display Options and press OK (**A**).

3. Move the Multi-selector down to select the Highlights option. Move the Multi-selector to the right to place a check mark next to the word Highlights (**B**).

4. Press OK on the Multi-selector to lock in your change.

A

B

Once the highlights warning is turned on, use it to check your images on the back of the LCD after taking a shot. If you see an area that is blinking, try setting exposure compensation to an underexposed setting like –1/3 or –2/3 stops and take another photo, checking the result on the screen. Don't make yourself crazy trying to get rid of every single blinking area. It is easy enough to add some black back into your photo later using post-editing software, and you don't want to underexpose the rest of the image because there is one blown-out highlight.

Sometimes, such as when you're shooting into the sun, the warning will blink no matter how much you adjust the exposure because there is just no detail in the highlight. On the contrary, if you're shooting a white wedding dress and the entire dress is blinking, then you have no detail in the dress and the bride will not be happy. Use your best judgment to determine if the warning is alerting you to an area where you want to retain highlight detail. If you are not sure what the perfect exposure is and you have to get a good shot, try bracketing your exposure. We will talk more about this in later chapters.

As you work your way through the coming chapters, you will see other tips and tricks to use in your daily photography, but the most important advice I can give is to take the time to understand the features of your camera so that you can leverage the technology in a knowledgeable way. This will pay off in better photographs.

Chapter 4 Assignments

This will be more of a mental challenge than anything else, but you should put a lot of work into these assignments, because the information covered in this chapter will define how you work with your camera from this point on. Granted, there may be times that you just want to grab some quick pictures and will resort to the automatic scene modes, but to get serious with your photography, you will want to learn the professional modes inside and out.

Starting off with Programmed Auto mode

Set your camera on P mode and start shooting. Become familiar with the adjustments you can make to your exposure by turning the main Command dial. Shoot in bright sun, deep shade, indoors, anywhere that you have different types and intensities of light. While you are shooting, make sure that you keep an eye on your ISO and raise or lower it according to your environment.

Learning to control time with Shutter Priority mode

Find some moving subjects and then set your camera to S mode. Have someone ride a bike back and forth or even just photograph cars as they go by. Start with a slow shutter speed of around 1/30 of a second, and then start shooting with faster and faster shutter speeds. Keep shooting until you can freeze the action.

Now find something that isn't moving, like a flower. Start with your shutter speed at something fast, like 1/500 of a second, and then work your way down. Don't brace the camera on a steady surface. Just try to shoot as slowly as possible, down to about 1/4 of a second. The point is to see how well you can handhold your camera before you start introducing hand shake into the image, making it appear soft and somewhat unfocused.

Controlling depth of field with Aperture Priority mode

The name of the game with Aperture Priority mode is depth of field. Set up three items at an equal distance from you, maybe chess pieces or something similar. Now set your zoom on a focal length of 50mm while focusing on the middle item. Set your camera to the largest aperture your lens will allow. Remember, large aperture means a low f-stop number like f/3.5, and small aperture means a high f-stop like f/22. Now take a photo. While still focusing on the middle subject, set your camera to the smallest aperture you lens will allow and take another photo. Now compare the depth of field between to the two images.

Giving and taking with Manual mode

Manual mode is not going to require a lot of work, but you should pay close attention to your results. Go outside on a sunny day and, using the camera in Manual mode, set your ISO to 100, your shutter speed to 1/125 of a second, and your aperture to f/16. Now press your shutter release button to get a meter reading. You should be pretty close to that zero mark. If not, make small adjustments to one of your settings until it hits that mark.

Here is where the fun begins. Start moving your shutter speed slower, to 1/60, and then set your aperture to f/22. Now go the other way. Set your aperture on f/8 and your shutter speed to 1/500. Review your images. If all went well, all the exposures should look the same. This is because you balanced the light with reciprocal changes to the aperture and shutter speed.

Now go back to our original setting of 1/125 at f/16 and try moving the shutter speed without changing the aperture. Just make 1/3-stop changes (1/125 to 1/100 to 1/80 to 1/60), and then review your images to see what a 1/3 stop of overexposure looks like. Then do the same thing going the opposite way. It's hard to know if you want to over- or underexpose a scene until you have actually done it and seen the results.

With each of the assignments, make sure that you keep track of your modes and exposures so that you can compare them with the image. If you are using software to review your images, you should also be able to check the camera settings that are embedded within the image's metadata.

Share your results with the book's Flickr group!
Join the group here: flickr.com/groups/nikond7100_fromsnapshotstogreatshots.

5

ENNIS, MT

VALLEY
LODGE
682-4264

LONGBRANCH
SALOON

SPORTSMANS
LODGE

ISO 125
1/800 sec.
f/5.6
70mm lens

Moving Target

HOW TO SHOOT WHEN YOUR SUBJECT IS IN MOTION

Now that you have learned about the professional modes, it's time to put your newfound knowledge to good use. Whether you are shooting the action at a professional sporting event or a child on a merry-go-round, you'll learn techniques that will help you bring out the best in your photography when your subject is in motion.

The number one thing to know when trying to capture a moving target is that speed is king! I'm not talking about how fast your subject is moving but rather how fast your shutter is opening and closing. Shutter speed is the key to freezing the moment in time—but also to conveying movement. It's all about intentions. If you want to freeze motion, then you'll want to use a fast shutter speed, but if you want to show motion, then you'll want to use a slower shutter speed. There are some other considerations for taking your shot to the next level, too: composition, lens selection, and a few more items that we will explore in this chapter. So strap on your seat belt and hit the gas, because here we go!

I processed this image using Nik Software's Color Efex Pro, adding contrast and structure to the image.

Shutter Priority used a higher f-stop of f/16 to achieve the desired 30-second exposure.

A cable release and a tripod are essential tools when trying to capture long exposures.

Often, I walk the city at night scouting out new locations for long-exposure opportunities. Near Chicago's North Shore Beach, there's a pedestrian overpass that crosses over the very hectic Lakeshore Drive, connecting Lincoln Park to the beach. This bridge provides a unique, relatively safe location for capturing Lakeshore Drive's crazy traffic with the iconic Chicago skyline as a backdrop. One of the nice things about night photography is it makes it easier to create a long exposure because the low light conditions require the shutter to stay open longer in order to create a proper exposure.

Motion blur is critical in helping to convey the sense of movement.

ISO 100
30 sec.
f/16
50mm lens

STOP RIGHT THERE!

Shutter speed is the main tool in the photographer's arsenal for capturing great action shots. The ability to freeze a moment in time often makes the difference between a good shot and a great one. To take advantage of this concept, you should have a solid grasp of the relationship between shutter speed and movement. When you press the shutter release button, your camera goes into action by opening the shutter curtain and then closing it after a predetermined length of time. The longer you leave your shutter open, the more your subject will move across the frame, so common sense dictates that the first thing to consider is just how fast your subject is moving.

Typically, you will be working in fractions of a second. How many fractions depends on several factors. Subject movement, while simple in concept, is actually based on three factors. The first is the direction of travel. Is the subject moving across your field of view (left to right) or traveling toward or away from you? The second consideration is the actual speed at which the subject is moving. There is a big difference between a moving sports car and a child on a bicycle. Finally, the distance from you to the subject has a direct bearing on how fast the action seems to be taking place. Let's take a brief look at each of these factors to see how they might affect your shooting.

DIRECTION OF TRAVEL

Typically, the first thing people think about when taking an action shot is how fast the subject is moving, but the first consideration should actually be the direction of travel. Where you are positioned in relation to the subject's direction of travel is critical in selecting the proper shutter speed. When you open your shutter, the lens gathers light from your subject and records it on the camera sensor. If the subject is moving across your viewfinder, you need a faster shutter speed to keep that lateral movement from being recorded as a streak across your image. Subjects that are moving perpendicular to your shooting location do not move across your viewfinder and appear to be more stationary. This allows you to use a slightly slower shutter speed (**Figure 5.1**). A subject that is moving in a diagonal direction—both across the frame and toward or away from you—requires a shutter speed in between the two.

FIGURE 5.1
Action coming toward the camera can be captured with slower shutter speeds. This Indian man was pushing his bicycle right at me. By photographing him head on, I not only froze the movement but the look on his face that showed how hard it was to push the heavy load.

SUBJECT SPEED

Once the angle of motion has been determined, you can then assess the speed at which the subject is traveling. The faster your subject moves, the faster your shutter speed needs to be in order to "freeze" that subject (**Figure 5.2**). A person walking across your frame might only require a shutter speed of 1/60 of a second, while a cyclist traveling in the same direction would call for 1/500 of a second. That same cyclist traveling toward you at the same rate of speed, rather than across the frame, might only require a shutter speed of 1/125 of a second. You can start to see how the relationship of speed and direction comes into play in your decision-making process.

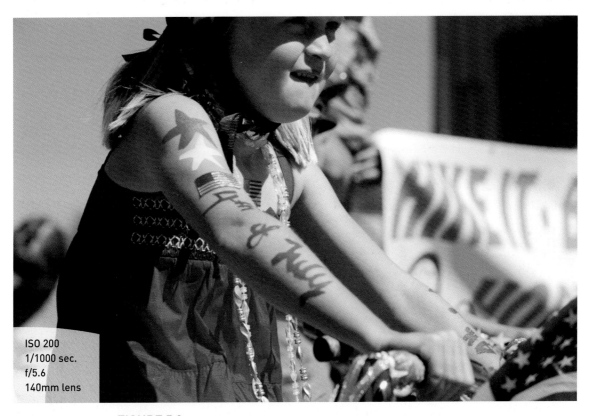

ISO 200
1/1000 sec.
f/5.6
140mm lens

FIGURE 5.2
Everyone loves a parade, and the key to getting good shots is shooting at a fast enough shutter speed to capture your favorite moments. Here I needed to increase my shutter speed to catch this young girl riding her bike across the frame.

SUBJECT-TO-CAMERA DISTANCE

So now we know both the direction and the speed of your subject. The final factor to address is the distance between you and the action. Picture yourself looking at a highway full of cars from up in a tall building a quarter of a mile from the road. As you stare down at the traffic moving along at 55 miles per hour, the cars and trucks seem to be slowly moving along the roadway. Now picture yourself standing in the median of that same road as the traffic flies by at the same rate of speed; it appears to be moving much faster.

Although the traffic is moving at the same speed, the shorter distance between you and the traffic makes the cars look as if they are moving much faster. This is because your field of view is much narrower; therefore, the subjects are not going to present themselves within the frame for the same length of time. The concept of distance applies to the length of your lens as well (**Figure 5.3**). If you are using a wide-angle lens, you can probably get away with a slower shutter speed than if you were using a telephoto, which puts you in the heart of the action. It all has to do with your field of view. That telephoto gets you "closer" to the action—and the closer you are, the faster your subject will be moving across your viewfinder.

FIGURE 5.3
Due to the distance of the subject from the camera, a slower shutter speed could be used to capture this action. For this dance recital, I was seated in the back of the auditorium, so a zoom lens with a faster shutter speed was required to capture the movement. This is a great example of using a high ISO to get a workable shutter speed.

ISO 6400
1/500 sec.
f/2.8
160mm lens

USING SHUTTER PRIORITY (S) MODE TO STOP MOTION

In Chapter 4, you were introduced to the professional shooting modes. As discussed there, the mode that gives you ultimate control over shutter speed is Shutter Priority, or S, mode, where you are responsible for selecting the shutter speed while handing over the aperture selection to the camera. The ability to concentrate on just one exposure factor helps you quickly make changes on the fly while staying glued to your viewfinder and your subject.

There are a couple of things to consider when using Shutter Priority mode, both of which have to do with the amount of light that is available when shooting. While you have control over which shutter speed you select in Shutter Priority mode, the range of shutter speeds that is available to you depends largely on how well lit your subject is lit.

ZOOM IN TO BE SURE

When reviewing your shots on the LCD, don't be fooled by the display. The smaller your image is, the sharper it will look. To ensure that you are getting sharp, blur-free images, make sure that you zoom in on your LCD.

To zoom in on your images, press the Playback button, located below the Mode dial on the left, and then press the Zoom In button to zoom (**Figure 5.4**). Continue pressing the Zoom In button to increase the zoom ratio.

To zoom back out, simply press the Zoom Out button (the magnifying glass with the minus sign on it) or press the Playback button again.

FIGURE 5.4
Zooming in on your image helps you confirm that the image is really sharp.

Playback

Zoom In

Typically, when shooting fast-paced action, you will be working with very fast shutter speeds. This means that your lens will probably be set to a large aperture. If the light is not sufficient for the shutter speed selected, you will need to do one of two things: Select a lens that offers a larger working aperture, or raise the ISO of the camera.

Working off the assumption that you have only one lens available, let's concentrate on balancing your exposure using the ISO.

Let's say that you are shooting a baseball game at night, and you want to get some great action shots. You set your camera to Shutter Priority mode and, after testing out some shutter speeds, determine that you need to shoot at 1/500 of a second to freeze the action on the field. When you place the viewfinder to your eye and press the shutter button halfway, you notice that the f-stop has been replaced by the word "Lo." This is your camera's way of telling you that the lens has now reached its maximum aperture and you are going to be underexposed if you shoot your pictures at the currently selected shutter speed. You could slow your shutter speed down until the Lo indicator goes away, but then you could get images with too much motion blur.

The alternative is to raise your ISO to a level that is fast enough for a proper exposure. The key here is to always use the lowest ISO that you can get away with. That might mean ISO 100 in bright sunny conditions or ISO 3200 for an indoor or night situation (**Figure 5.5**).

ISO 800
1/320 sec.
f/1.2
85mm lens

FIGURE 5.5
While in India I had a chance to photograph a Kushti wrestling match, which is a traditional style of wrestling performed in a dirt ring. This particular match was being performed in a poorly lit room, so I increased my ISO to 800 and shot wide open at an f/1.2 aperture in hopes of freezing the fast movements of the wrestlers.

Just remember that the higher the ISO, the greater the amount of noise in your image. This is the reason that you see professional sports photographers using those mammoth lenses perched atop a monopod: They could use a smaller lens, but to get a very large aperture they need a huge piece of glass on the front of the lens. The larger the glass on the front of the lens, the more light it gathers, and the larger the aperture for shooting. For the working pro, the large aperture translates into low ISO (and thus low noise), fast shutter speeds, and razor-sharp action. But, you're in luck: The D7100 has a very low noise at higher ISO, so feel free to increase the ISO so you can get those shots you might otherwise miss.

ADJUSTING YOUR ISO ON THE FLY

1. Look at the exposure values (the shutter speed and aperture settings) in the lower portion of your viewfinder.

2. If you're unable to achieve a fast shutter speed, then it's time to increase the ISO.

3. Select the higher ISO by observing the control panel (**A**) while pressing and holding the ISO button on the back of the camera and rotating the main Command dial to the right. Once the desired ISO is selected, simply release the ISO button (**B**).

4. Now observe the shutter speed and Exposure indicator to determine if the desired speed and exposure have been achieved. Repeat steps 2–4 until optimum speeds and exposure have been achieved.

A

B

USING APERTURE PRIORITY (A) MODE TO ISOLATE YOUR SUBJECT

One of the benefits of working in Shutter Priority mode with fast shutter speeds is that, more often than not, you will be shooting with the largest aperture available on your lens. Shooting with a large aperture allows you to use faster shutter speeds, but it also narrows your depth of field.

To isolate your subject in order to focus your viewer's attention on it, a larger aperture is required. The larger aperture reduces the foreground and background sharpness: The larger the aperture, the more blurred the foreground and background will be.

The reason that I bring this up here is that when you are shooting most sporting events, the idea is to isolate your main subject by having it in focus while the rest of the image has some amount of blur. This sharp focus draws your viewer right to the subject. Studies have shown that the eye is drawn to sharp areas before moving on to the blurry ones. Also, depending on what your subject matter is, a busy background can be distracting if everything in the photo is equally sharp. If you haven't used a narrow depth of field, it might be difficult for the viewer to establish exactly what the main subject is in your picture.

Let's look at how to use depth of field to bring focus to your subject. In the previous section, I told you that you should use Shutter Priority mode for getting those really fast shutter speeds to stop action. Generally speaking, Shutter Priority mode will be the mode you most often use for shooting sports and other action, but at times you'll want to ensure that you are getting the narrowest depth of field possible in your image. The way to do this is by using Aperture Priority mode, or A.

So how do you know when you should use Aperture Priority mode as opposed to Shutter Priority mode? There's no simple answer, but your LCD can help you make this determination. The best scenario for using Aperture Priority mode is a brightly lit scene where maximum apertures will still give you plenty of shutter speed to stop the action.

Let's say that you are shooting a soccer game in the midday sun. If you have determined that you need something between 1/500 and 1/1250 of a second for stopping the action, you could just set your camera to a high shutter speed in Shutter Priority mode and start shooting. But you also want to be using an aperture of, say, f/4.5 to get that narrow depth of field. Here's the problem: If you set your camera to Shutter Priority mode and select 1/1000 of a second as a nice compromise, you might get that desired f-stop—but you might not. As the meter is trained on your moving subject, the light levels could rise or fall, which might actually change that desired f-stop to something higher like f/5.6 or even f/8. Now the depth of field is extended, and you will no longer get that nice isolation and separation that you wanted.

To rectify this, switch the camera to Aperture Priority mode and select f/4.5 as your aperture. Now, as you begin shooting, the camera holds that aperture and makes exposure adjustments with the shutter speed. As I said before, this works well when you have lots of light—enough light so that you can have a high enough shutter speed without introducing motion blur.

THE ISO SENSITIVITY AUTO CONTROL TRICK

There is a very cool trick that can get you the best of both worlds and that won't sacrifice your shutter speed or aperture. With the ISO Sensitivity auto control feature, you can set the camera to automatically select an ISO that keeps you at your preferred shutter speed, while using the largest aperture and lowest ISO possible. It will also put an upper limit on the ISO to keep you from getting too much noise in your images; but, as I mentioned before, the D7100 has some of the best low-noise performance on the market.

Here's the way it works. If I am shooting an activity that requires a shutter speed of 1/250 of a second, I set that as the minimum in the auto control settings. Then I decide that I can deal with the noise that is produced with an ISO up to 3200, so I set that as my maximum sensitivity. Since I would always like to use the lowest ISO, I set the low ISO sensitivity to 100. Once everything is set, the camera will now adjust my ISO without any interaction from me, letting me shoot at my desired shutter speed at the lowest possible ISO and largest aperture setting possible.

SETTING UP THE ISO SENSITIVITY AUTO CONTROL FEATURE

1. Press the Menu button and then use the Multi-selector to scroll down to the Shooting menu.

2. Press the OK button on the Multi-selector to enter the menu and then locate the ISO Sensitivity Settings feature (**A**).

3. Press the Multi-selector to the right to enter the setup screen.

4. Press OK on the Multi-selector to select the lowest ISO that you wish to use (ISO Sensitivity) and press the OK button (**B**).

5. Press the Multi-selector down to highlight Auto ISO Sensitivity Control and then select On to activate the feature (C).

B

C

6. Use the Multi-selector to choose Maximum Sensitivity (D). This will be the upper limit of your ISO.

7. Finally, select the Minimum shutter speed that you want to use while shooting (E). This will be completely dependent on the speed necessary to stop the action you are shooting.

D

E

With everything set up, you can begin shooting without fear of constantly having to change the ISO. This technique is also quite helpful when working in varying light conditions. As you are shooting, you will notice the ISO Auto warning in the lower right portion of the viewfinder along with the adjusted ISO setting.

KEEP THEM IN FOCUS WITH CONTINUOUS-SERVO FOCUS AND AF FOCUS POINT SELECTION

With the exposure issue handled for the moment, let's move on to something equally important: focusing. If you have browsed your manual, you know that you have several focus modes to choose from in the D7100. To get the greatest benefit from each of them, it is important to understand how they work and the situations in which each mode will give you the best opportunity to grab a great shot. Because we are discussing subject movement, our first choice is going to be Continuous-servo AF mode (AF-C). AF-C mode uses all of the focus points in the camera to find a moving subject and then lock in the focus when the shutter button is completely depressed.

SELECTING AND SHOOTING IN CONTINUOUS-SERVO AF FOCUS MODE

1. Press and hold the AF button while observing the control panel (**A**).
2. Now rotate the main Command dial while continuing to hold the AF button. Once you have selected AF-C, release the AF button (**B**).
3. The camera will maintain the subject's focus as long as it remains within one of the focus points in the viewfinder or until you release the shutter button or take a picture.

A

B

Note that holding down the shutter button for long periods of time will cause your battery to drain much faster because the camera will be constantly focusing on the subject.

When using the AF-C mode, you can use the AF point mode set to Dynamic Area, which makes a focus point of your choosing the primary focus but uses information from the surrounding points if your subject happens to move away from the point.

1. To set the AF-area mode, press and hold the AF button on the front of the camera while observing the control panel (**A**).

A

2. Now rotate the Sub-command dial while holding the AF button (**B**). As you turn the dial, your AF modes will be displayed on the control panel. Select from one of three dynamic modes and release the AF button when you have made your selection (**C**).

B

C

Note that the AF mode is used to select the method with which the camera will focus the lens. This is different from the AF point, which is a cluster of small points that are visible in the viewfinder and are used to determine where you want the lens to focus.

STOP AND GO WITH 3D-TRACKING AF

If you are going to be changing between a moving target and one that is still, you should consider using the 3D-tracking AF mode. The 3D mode uses a color signature to help track the subject with the help of all 51 AF points. This system works very well when the subject's color is different from that of the background.

When you have a stationary subject, simply place your selected focus point on your subject and the camera will focus on it. If your subject begins to move out of focus, the camera will track the movement, keeping a sharp focus.

For example, suppose you are shooting a football game. The quarterback has brought the team to the line and he is standing behind the center, waiting for the ball to be hiked. If you are using the 3D-tracking AF mode, you can place your focus point on the quarterback and start taking pictures of him as he stands at the line. As soon as the ball is hiked and the action starts, the camera will switch to tracking mode and follow his movement within the frame. This can be a little tricky at first, but once you master it, it will make your action shooting effortless.

To select 3D-tracking, simply follow the same steps listed for selecting dynamic modes but instead select the 3D-tracking mode. It is important to know that the 3D-tracking AF mode uses color and contrast to locate and then follow the subject, so this mode might be less effective when everything is similar in tone or color.

CHOOSING A FOCUS MODE

Selecting the proper focus mode depends largely on what type of subject you are photographing. Single Point is typically best for stationary subjects. It allows you to determine exactly where you want your focus to be and then recompose your image while holding the focus in place. If you are taking pictures of an active subject who is moving quickly, trying to set a focus point with Single Point can be difficult, if not impossible. This is when you will want to rely on the Dynamic Area and 3D-tracking modes to quickly assess the subject distance and set your lens focus. This can be especially helpful if the subject distance is varying constantly.

MANUAL FOCUS FOR ANTICIPATED ACTION

While I use the automatic focus modes for the majority of my shooting, there are times when I like to fall back on manual focus. This is usually when I know when and where the action will occur and I want to capture the subject as it crosses a certain plane of focus. This is useful in sports like motocross or auto racing, where the subjects are on a defined track and I know exactly where I want to capture the action. I could try tracking the subject, but sometimes the view can be obscured by a curve. By prefocusing the camera, all I have to do is wait for the subject to approach my point of focus (**Figure 5.6**) and then start firing the camera.

ISO 400
1/200 sec.
f/4
280mm lens

FIGURE 5.6
Anticipating where
your subject will be
is a major advan-
tage when captur-
ing motion.

It is also a good idea to decide how much of the environment you want to show in your image. With these twins riding the tandem bicycle, I wanted to show the old-fashioned buildings in the background to give a sense of Mackinac Island. I could have cropped in tighter, but I would have lost the essential background information (**Figure 5.7**).

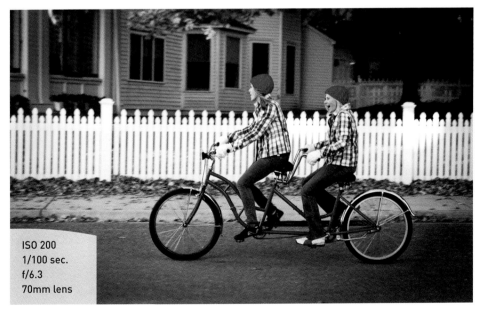

ISO 200
1/100 sec.
f/6.3
70mm lens

FIGURE 5.7
You don't always
need to crop in tight
on a motion shot.
By showing more of
the environment, I
was able to give the
viewer a sense of
time and place.

DRIVE MODES

The drive mode determines how fast your camera will take pictures. Single Frame is for taking one photograph at a time. With every full press of the shutter release button, the camera will take a single image. The continuous modes allow for a more rapid capture rate. Think of it like a machine gun. When you are using one of the continuous modes, the camera will continue to take pictures as long as the shutter release button is held down.

KEEPING UP WITH THE CONTINUOUS SHOOTING MODES

Getting great focus is one thing, but capturing the best moment on the sensor can be difficult if you are shooting just one frame at a time. In the world of sports, and in life in general, things move pretty fast. If you blink, you might miss it. The same can be said for shooting in Single Frame mode. Fortunately, your D7100 comes equipped with a Continuous High (CH) shooting—or "burst"—mode that lets you capture a series of images at up to six frames a second (**Figure 5.8**). You can also select Continuous Low (CL), which allows the user to customize the desired frames per second by using the Custom Settings.

SETTING UP AND SHOOTING IN CONTINUOUS SHOOTING MODE

While pressing the Release Mode dial lock simply turn the Release Mode dial to either CL or CH. CH will provide up to six frames per second, and CL will provide one to five frames per second, based upon the user's preference. To set up CL, go to D6 in your Custom Settings menu. (For more on this, refer to page 239 of your user manual.)

A

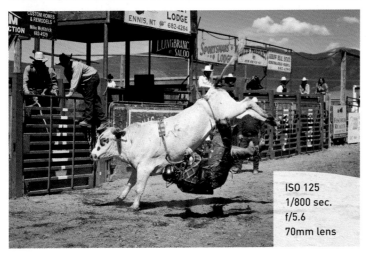

ISO 125
1/800 sec.
f/5.6
70mm lens

FIGURE 5.8

Using continuous mode means that you are sure to capture the peak of the action. Using the continuous shooting mode causes the camera to keep taking images for as long as you hold down the shutter release button. In Single Frame mode, you have to release the button and then press it again to take another picture.

Your camera has an internal memory, called a buffer, where images are stored while they are being processed prior to being moved to your memory card. Depending on the image format you are using, the buffer might fill up, and the camera will stop shooting until space is made in the buffer for new images. The camera readout in the viewfinder tells you how many frames you have available in burst mode. Just look in the viewfinder at the bottom right to see the maximum number of images for burst shooting. As you shoot, the number will go down, and then back up as the images are written to the memory card.

A SENSE OF MOTION

Shooting action isn't always about freezing the action. At times you want to convey a sense of motion so that the viewer can get a feel for the movement and flow of an event. Two techniques you can use to achieve this effect are panning and motion blur.

PANNING

Panning has been used for decades to capture the speed of a moving object as it moves across the frame. It doesn't work well for subjects that are moving toward or away from you. Panning is achieved by following your subject across your frame, moving your camera along with the subject, and using a slower-than-normal shutter speed so that the background (and sometimes even a bit of the subject) has a sideways blur but the main portion of your subject is sharp and blur-free.

The key to a great panning shot is selecting the right shutter speed: too fast and you won't get the desired blurring of the background; too slow and the subject will be too blurry and will not be recognizable. Practice the technique until you can achieve a smooth motion with your camera that follows along with your subject. The other thing to remember when panning is to follow through even after the shutter has closed. This will keep the motion smooth and give you better images.

Panning can take a lot of practice before you stumble upon the correct shutter speed. During the Chicago Marathon I was able to take several practice shots of the wheelchair division as the competitors crossed my path. The speeds achieved by the athletes were incredibly fast, so it took several test shots before I was able to dial in the appropriate shutter speed. Aided by continuous mode and Shutter Priority, I was able to achieve the perfect shot (**Figure 5.9**), albeit through trial and error.

ISO 320
1/40 sec.
f/7.1
200mm lens

FIGURE 5.9
Following the subject as it moves across your field of view allows for a slower shutter speed and adds a sense of motion. Panning takes practice, so it's helpful to seek out plenty of opportunities to hone your skills.

MOTION BLUR

Another way to let the viewer in on the feel of the action is to simply include some blur in the image (**Figure 5.10**). This isn't accidental blur from choosing the wrong shutter speed. This blur is more exaggerated, and it tells a story (**Figure 5.11**). In Figure 5.10, I wanted to capture the strumming of the guitar player's hand. I felt that the motion of the hand told a better story than simply freezing the motion.

ISO 4000
1/25 sec.
f/3.5
105mm lens

FIGURE 5.10
The movement of the hand strumming the guitar coupled with a slower shutter speed conveys a sense of motion.

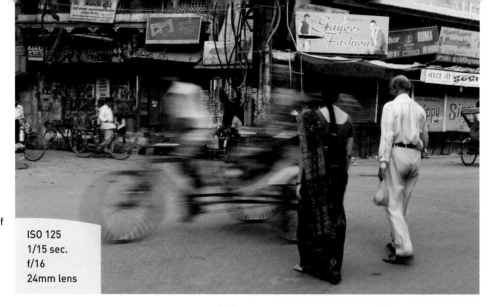

ISO 125
1/15 sec.
f/16
24mm lens

Just as in panning, there is no preordained shutter speed to use for this effect. It is simply a matter of trial and error until you have a look that conveys the action. I try to show an area of the frame that is frozen—for instance, in the previous shot of the musician, the guitar may be frozen or still, but the hand is moving. In the shot of the couple in **Figure 5.12**, the couple has paused momentarily. This helps lend visual contrast and adds to the story of the photo. The key to this technique is the correct shutter speed combined with keeping the camera still during the exposure. You are trying to capture the motion of the subject, not the photographer or the camera, so use a good shooting stance or even a tripod.

ISO 125
1/15 sec.
f/16
24mm lens

TIPS FOR SHOOTING ACTION
GIVE THEM SOMEWHERE TO GO

Framing your image is as important as how well you expose it. A poorly composed shot can ruin a great moment by not holding the viewer's attention.

One common mistake in action photography is not using the frame properly. If you are dealing with a subject moving horizontally across your field of view, give the subject somewhere to go by placing it to the side of the frame, with its motion leading toward the middle of the frame (**Figure 5.13**). This offsetting of the subject will introduce a sense of direction and anticipation for the viewer. Unless you are going to completely fill the image with the action, try to avoid placing your subject in the middle of the frame.

Here I was photographing the demolition of the famous Cabrini Green housing projects in Chicago. The debris was flying off the building every time the wrecking ball hit the structure. Framing the image this way shows you how far the debris was flying and guides your eye through the movement.

FIGURE 5.13
Try to leave space in front of your subject to lead the action in a direction. In this case, the bright blue sky provided the negative space to show the directionality of the flying debris.

ISO 125
1/250 sec.
f/11
80mm lens

GET IN FRONT OF THE ACTION

Here's another tip. When shooting action, show the action coming toward you (**Figure 5.14**) rather than going away from you. People want to see faces. Faces convey the action, the drive, the sense of urgency, and the emotion of the moment. So if you are shooting action involving people, always position yourself so that the action is either coming at you or is at least perpendicular to your position.

ISO 200
1/250 sec.
f/3.2
148mm lens

FIGURE 5.14
Shooting from the front with a telephoto gives a feeling that the action is coming right at you. You can see the cyclist blowing his whistle, which draws you in to the feeling of the scene. You also get a real perspective on the wheelchair athletes and their determination as they are rounding this corner in the Chicago Marathon.

PUT YOUR CAMERA IN A DIFFERENT PLACE

Changing your vantage point is a great way to find new angles. Shooting from above with a wide-angle lens might let you incorporate some depth into the image. Shooting from farther away with a telephoto lens will compress the elements in a scene and allow you to crop in tighter on the action. Don't be afraid to experiment and try new things.

The image in **Figure 5.15** revealed the Kushti wrestlers from a different viewpoint. Instead of seeing them straight on, the viewer has a higher vantage point, which shows a new take on their exercise routine.

I could not have achieved this viewpoint if I had not climbed up to this higher vantage point. I wanted to get a shot that showed all of the wrestlers warming up, so I climbed up on top of a cement embankment. If I had stayed below, the image would have been at eye level, and the depth of the shot would have been missing. I also would not have been able to capture as many wrestlers in the frame with an eye-level vantage point. Sometimes a low perspective works fine, but also look up to see if you can get to high ground for a better view.

FIGURE 5.15
Putting your camera in a different place can yield pleasing results.

ISO 500
1/8000 sec.
f/28
18mm lens

Chapter 5 Assignments

The mechanics of motion

For this first assignment, you need to find some action. Explore the relationship between the speed of an object and its direction of travel. Use the same shutter speed to record your subject moving toward you and across your view. Try using the same shutter speed for both to compare the difference made by the direction of travel.

Wide vs. telephoto

Just as with the first assignment, photograph a subject moving in different directions, but this time, use a wide-angle lens and then a telephoto. Check out how the telephoto setting on the zoom lens will require faster shutter speeds than the lens at its wide-angle setting.

Getting a feel for focusing modes

We discussed two different ways to autofocus for action: Dynamic Area and 3D-tracking. Starting with Dynamic Area mode, find a moving subject and use the mode to get familiar with the way the mode works.

Now repeat the process using the 3D-tracking AF mode. The point of the exercise is to become familiar enough with the two modes to decide which one to use for the situation you are photographing.

Anticipating the spot using manual focus

For this assignment, you will need to find a subject that you know will cross a specific line that you can prefocus on. A street with moderate traffic works well for this. Focus on a spot on the street that the cars will travel across (don't forget to set your lens for manual focus). To do this right, you need to set the drive mode on the camera to continuous mode. Now, when a car approaches the spot, start shooting. Try shooting in three- or four-frame bursts.

Following the action

Panning is a great way to show motion. To begin, find a subject that will move across your path at a steady speed and practice following it in your viewfinder from side to side. Now, with the camera in Shutter Priority mode, set your shutter speed to 1/30 of a second and the focus mode to Dynamic Area. Now pan along with the subject and shoot as it moves across your view. Experiment with different shutter speeds and focal lengths. Panning is one of those skills that take some time to get a feel for, so try it with different types of subjects moving at different speeds.

Feeling the movement

Instead of panning with the motion, use a stationary camera position and adjust the shutter speed until you get a blurred effect that gives the sense of motion while the subject is still identifiable. There is a big difference between a slightly blurred photo that looks like you just picked the wrong shutter speed and one that looks as if it intends to show motion. As with panning, it will take some experimentation to find just the right shutter speed to achieve the desired effect.

Share your results with the book's Flickr group!
Join the group here: flickr.com/groups/nikond7100_fromsnapshotstogreatshots.

6

ISO 160
1/800 sec.
f/3.2
35mm lens

Perfect Portraits

SETTINGS AND FEATURES TO MAKE GREAT PORTRAITS

One of my favorite things to do while traveling is take portraits. I find that people are very approachable if you are sincere and respect their wishes. Taking pictures of people is one of the great joys of photography. You will experience a tremendous sense of accomplishment when you capture the spirit and personality of someone in a photograph. In this chapter, we will explore some camera features and techniques that can help you create great portraits.

PORING OVER THE PICTURE

If you ever visit Kenya, then you must consider visiting a Masai village. The Masai people are very friendly, and their way of life is fascinating. Several years ago I toured a Masai village and learned about their culture and strong sense of community. The photo opportunities were endless, but the real treasure came in getting to know the people.

Using a large aperture combined with a high ISO allowed me to increase my shutter speed so that I could hand-hold the shot.

I turned my flash off to create a natural-looking image.

I chose to frame the image with emphasis placed on the smoke while focusing on the Masai's hands.

ISO 1600
1/500 sec.
f/3.2
85mm lens

AUTOMATIC PORTRAIT MODE

In Chapter 3, we reviewed all of the automatic scene modes. One of them, Portrait mode, is dedicated to shooting portraits. While this is not my preferred camera setting, it is a great jumping-off point for those who are just starting out. The key to using this mode is to understand what is going on with the camera so that when you venture further into portrait photography, you can expand on the settings and get the most from your camera and, more importantly, your subject.

Whether you are photographing an individual or a group, the emphasis should always be on the subject. Portrait mode uses a larger aperture setting to keep the depth of field very narrow, which means that the background will appear slightly blurred or out of focus. To take full advantage of this effect, use a medium- to telephoto-length lens. Also, keep a pretty close distance to your subject. If you shoot from too far away, the narrow depth of field will not be as effective.

USING APERTURE PRIORITY MODE

If you took a poll of portrait photographers to see which shooting mode was most often used for portraits, the answer would certainly be Aperture Priority (A, for short) mode. Selecting the right aperture is important for placing the most critically sharp area of the photo on your subject while simultaneously blurring all of the distracting background clutter (**Figure 6.1**). Not only will a large aperture give the narrowest depth of field, it will also allow you to shoot in lower light levels at lower ISO settings.

This isn't to say that you have to use the largest aperture on your lens. An aperture of f/1.2 may be too large, thus creating a shallow depth of field. A good place to begin is f/5.6. This will give you enough depth of field to keep the entire face in focus, while providing enough blur to eliminate distractions in the background. Remember, a portrait is all about the eyes, so focus first on the eyes and recompose the frame if needed (**Figure 6.2**). This isn't a hard-and-fast setting; it's just a good, all-around number to start with. Your aperture might change depending on the focal length of the lens you are using and on the amount of blur that you want for your foreground and background elements.

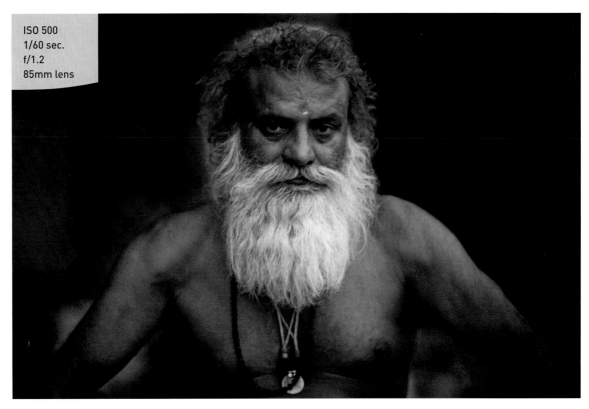

ISO 500
1/60 sec.
f/1.2
85mm lens

FIGURE 6.1
Using a wide aperture, especially with a longer lens, blurs distracting background details.

ISO 800
1/50 sec.
f/2.8
70mm lens

FIGURE 6.2
Try to connect with the person when you're taking her photograph. You don't want her looking away; you want to maintain a good focus on the eyes.

GO WIDE FOR ENVIRONMENTAL PORTRAITS

There will be times when your subject's environment is of great significance to the story you want to tell. This might mean using a smaller aperture to get more detail in the background or foreground. Once again, by using Aperture Priority mode, you can set your aperture to a higher f-stop, such as f/8 or f/11, and include the important details of the scene that surrounds your subject.

FIGURE 6.3
I like to take two shots whenever I'm photograph-ing a scene where the environment is key, a wide shot and a tight close-up. A wide-angle lens allows you to capture more of the environment in the scene without hav-ing to increase the distance between you and the subject.

Using a wider-than-normal lens can also assist in getting more depth of field, as well as showing the surrounding area. A wide-angle lens requires less stopping down of the aperture (making the aperture smaller) to achieve an acceptable depth of field. This is because wide-angle lenses cover a greater area, so the depth of field appears to cover a greater percentage of the scene.

A wider lens might also be necessary to relay more information about the scenery (**Figure 6.3**). Select a lens length that is wide enough to tell the story but not so wide that you distort the subject. Few things in the world of portraiture are quite as unflattering as giving someone a big, distorted nose (unless you are going for that sort of look). When shooting a portrait with a wide-angle lens, keep the subject away from the edge of the frame. This will reduce the distortion, especially in very wide focal lengths. As the lens length increases, distortion will be reduced.

ISO 800
1/60 sec.
f/2.8
24mm lens

There are multiple metering modes in your camera, but the way they all work is very similar. A light meter measures the amount of light being reflected off your subject and then renders a suggested exposure value based on the brightness of the subject and the ISO setting of the sensor. To establish this value, the meter averages all of the brightness values to come up with a middle tone, sometimes referred to as 18 percent gray. The exposure value is then rendered based on this middle gray value. This means that a white wall would be underexposed and a black wall would be overexposed in an effort to make each one appear gray. To assist with special lighting situations, the D7100 has three metering modes: Matrix (**Figure 6.4**), which uses the entire frame; Spot (**Figure 6.5**), which takes specific readings from small areas (often used with a gray card); and Center-weighted (**Figure 6.6**), which looks at the entire frame but places most of the exposure emphasis on the center of the frame.

FIGURE 6.4
The Matrix Metering mode uses the entire frame.

FIGURE 6.5
The Spot Metering mode uses a very small area of the frame.

FIGURE 6.6
The Center-weighted Metering mode looks at the entire frame but emphasizes the center of it.

METERING MODES FOR PORTRAITS

For many portrait situations, the Matrix Metering mode will work great. (For more on how metering works, see the "Metering Basics" sidebar, above) This mode measures light values from all portions of the viewfinder and then establishes a proper exposure for the scene. The only problem that you might encounter when using this metering mode is when you have very light or dark backgrounds in your portrait shots.

In these instances, the meter might be fooled into using the wrong exposure information because it will be trying to lighten or darken the entire scene based on the prominence of dark or light areas (**Figure 6.7**). You can deal with this in one of two ways. You can use the Exposure Compensation feature, which we cover in Chapter 7, to dial in adjustments for over- and underexposure. Or you can change the metering mode to Center-weighted Metering. The Center-weighted Metering mode uses only the center area of the viewfinder (about 9 percent) to get its exposure information. This is the best way to achieve proper exposure for most portraits; metering off skin tones, averaged with hair and clothing, will often give a more accurate exposure (**Figure 6.8**). This metering mode is also great to use when the subject is strongly backlit.

FIGURE 6.7
The light background color and clothing fooled the meter into choosing a slightly underexposed setting for the photo.

FIGURE 6.8
When I switched to the Center-weighted Metering mode, my camera was able to ignore much of the background and add a little more time to the exposure.

ISO 100
1/80 sec.
f/5.6
40mm lens

ISO 100
1/40 sec.
f/5.6
40mm lens

SETTING YOUR METERING MODE TO CENTER-WEIGHTED METERING

1. Press and hold the meter button located at the top right side of your camera.

2. While holding the meter button, rotate the main Command dial to locate the Center-weighted Metering icon and release the meter button once you've selected it (**A**).

A

3. By default, your camera is set to calculate your center weight, with an emphasis on an 8mm center circle. You can reduce or expand that center circle via the Custom Setting menu B4 (**B**).

USING THE AE LOCK (AUTO EXPOSURE LOCK) FEATURE

Often, your subject won't be in the center of the frame but you'll still want to use the Center-weighted Metering mode. So how can you get an accurate reading if the subject isn't in the center? Try using the Auto Exposure Lock feature to hold the exposure setting while you recompose.

AE Lock lets you use the exposure setting from any portion of the scene that you think is appropriate, and then lock that setting in regardless of how the scene looks when you recompose. An example of this would be when you're shooting a photograph of someone and a large amount of blue sky appears in the picture. Normally, the meter might be fooled by all that bright sky and try to reduce the exposure. Using AE Lock, you can establish the correct metering by zooming in on the subject (or even pointing the camera toward the ground), taking the meter reading and locking it in with AE Lock feature, and then recomposing and taking your photo with the locked-in exposure.

SHOOTING WITH THE AE LOCK FEATURE

1. Find the AE-L/AF-L button (which we'll call AE-L for short) on the back of the camera and place your thumb on it.

2. While looking through the viewfinder, place the focus point on your subject, press the shutter release button halfway to get a meter reading, and focus the camera.

3. Press and hold the AE-L button to lock in the meter reading. You should see the AE-L indicator in the viewfinder.

4. While pressing the AE-L button, recompose your shot and take the photo.

5. To take more than one photo without having to take another meter reading, just hold down the AE-L button until you are done using the meter setting.

6. Remember, if you're using autofocus, then the focus and the meter reading will be locked simultaneously.

FOCUSING: THE EYES HAVE IT

It has been said that the eyes are the windows to the soul, and nothing could be truer when you are photographing someone (**Figure 6.9**). You could have the perfect composition and exposure, but if the eyes aren't sharp the entire image suffers. While there are many focusing modes to choose from on your D7100 for portrait work, you can't beat AF-S (Single-servo AF) mode using a single focusing point. AF-S focusing will establish a single focus for the lens and then hold it until you take the photograph; the other focusing modes continue focusing until the photograph is taken. The single-point selection lets you place the focusing point right on your subject's eye and set that spot as the critical focus spot. Using AF-S mode lets you get that focus and recompose all in one motion.

ISO 400
1/160 sec.
f/2.8
70mm lens

FIGURE 6.9
When photographing people, you should almost always place the emphasis on the eyes.

SETTING YOUR FOCUS TO A SINGLE POINT

1. Press and hold the Focus Mode selector, near the lens on the front of the camera (**A**).

2. While holding the button, rotate the Sub-command dial with your index finger.

3. Select the Single Point icon on the control panel and release the Focus Mode selector button (**B**).

A   B

SETTING UP FOR AF-S FOCUS MODE

1. Press and hold the Focus Mode selector, near the lens on the front of the camera.

2. While holding the button, rotate the main Command dial with your thumb.

3. Release the Focus Mode selector when AF-S is displayed in the control panel (**B**, above).

4. When you are back in shooting mode, use the Multi-selector to move the focus point to one of the 51 available positions. The AF points are visible while you are looking through the viewfinder or may be selected while you are viewing the information display. To view in the information display, simply press the Info button on the back of the camera to activate it.

Now, to shoot using this focus point, place that point on one of your subject's eyes, and press the shutter button halfway until you hear or see the focus indicator chirp. While still holding the shutter button down halfway, recompose if necessary and take your shot.

I typically use the center point for focus selection. I find it easier to place that point directly on the location where my critical focus should be established and then recompose the shot. Even though the single point can be selected from any of the focus points, it typically takes longer to figure out where that point should be in relation to my subject. By using the center point, I can quickly establish focus and get on with my shooting.

CLASSIC BLACK-AND-WHITE PORTRAITS

There is something timeless about a black-and-white portrait. It eliminates the distraction of color and puts all the emphasis on the subject. To visualize in black and white without having to resort to any image-processing software, set your picture control to Monochrome (**Figure 6.10**).

The picture controls are automatically applied when shooting with the JPEG file format; this means the black-and-white image will be created in camera. If you are shooting in RAW, the picture that displays on your rear LCD is a low-resolution JPEG file that mimics what the RAW file will look like once converted in software. Keep in mind, the RAW file that you import from your camera will always contain the color information recorded at time of capture. The RAW file will need to be further converted into a black-and-white image using an application such as Adobe Lightroom, Adobe Photoshop, or Apple Aperture. The advantage to shooting in RAW is that you're able to produce a color image from the original RAW file when desired, plus you now have the ability to produce a black-and-white image. Additionally, you maintain the ability to use color channels to make further adjustments to the black-and-white image. I could go on and on because I love black and white, but to learn more about my process, consider picking up a copy of *Black and White: From Snapshots to Great Shots.*

When shooting RAW, the real key to using the Monochrome picture control is to help you visualize what your image will look like once it's converted to black and white. Another advantage to using the camera's built-in Monochrome setting is the ability to create filter effects even if you don't have a lens-mounted filter. A red filter will typically lighten skin tones, a yellow filter will darken skies, an orange filter will create contrast in many landscape images, and a green filter will darken reds and lighten greens such as grass.

ISO 500
1/60 sec.
f/1.4
35mm lens

THE PORTRAIT PICTURE CONTROL FOR BETTER SKIN TONES

As long as we are talking about picture controls for portraits, there is another control on your D7100 that has been tuned specifically for this type of shooting. Oddly enough, it's called Portrait. To set this control on your camera, simply follow the same directions as earlier, except this time, select the Portrait control (PT) instead of Monochrome. There are individual options for the Portrait control which, like the Monochrome control, include sharpness and contrast. You can also change the saturation (how intense the colors will be) and hue, which lets you change the skin tones from more reddish to more yellowish.

My recommendation is that you do most of your adjustments to contrast, saturation, and hue in post-processing. Once again, this is not an issue for RAW file shooters, because a RAW file is the digital equivalent of a negative and can be manipulated over and over without any harmful effects. However, as a JPEG shooter, tinkering does pose as a problem, because the in-camera settings are permanently applied to the image. That doesn't mean that you can't convert a JPEG file to black and white or reduce sharpening during the post-processing state. You can, but not with the same level of quality that you get with a RAW file.

DETECT FACES WITH LIVE VIEW

Facial detection is becoming commonplace in digital cameras. Your D7100 has four autofocus modes for Live View: Wide Area AF, Normal Area AF, Subject Tracking AF, and Face Priority AF. These modes are different from the standard modes like AF-S, AF-C, and AF-A. Face Priority mode is probably the slowest of the Live View focusing modes, so use it with a tripod or when your subjects are going to remain fairly still. When you turn on Live View with Face Priority focusing, the camera does an amazing thing: It zeroes in on any face appearing on the LCD and places a box around it. I'm not sure how it works; it just does.

There is a whole chapter in your manual that is dedicated to using Live View mode, starting on page 153.

1. Activate Live View by pressing the LV button. Next, Press the AF mode button and rotate the Sub-command dial to the desired AF-area mode.

2. Point your camera at a person and watch as the yellow frame appears over the face in the LCD.

3. Depress and hold the shutter release button halfway to focus on the face and wait until you hear the confirmation chirp.

4. Press the shutter button fully to take the photograph.

USE FILL FLASH FOR REDUCING SHADOWS

A common problem when taking pictures of people outside, especially during the midday hours, is that the overhead sun can create dark shadows under the eyes and chin. You could have your subject turn his or her face to the sun, but that is usually considered cruel and unusual punishment. So how can you have your subject's back to the sun and still get a decent exposure of the face? Try turning on your flash to fill in the shadows.

This also works well when you are photographing someone wearing a cap (**Figure 6.11**). The bill of the hat tends to create heavy shadows over the eyes, and the fill flash will lighten up those areas while providing a really nice catchlight in the eyes.

ISO 100
1/320 sec.
f/8
85mm lens

FIGURE 6.11
I used fill flash here to fill in the shadows created by the bull rider's cowboy hat. The flash does not completely remove the shadow, because that would look unnatural and be an overexposed image, but it helps fill in the darkest shadows. Here I wanted the bull rider to have his back to the fence, so instead of repositioning him, I just used fill flash.

The key to using the flash as a fill is to not use it on full power. If you do, the camera will try to balance the flash with the daylight, and you will get a flat and feature-less face.

CATCHLIGHT

A *catchlight* is that little sparkle that adds life to the eyes and brings attention to them. When you are photographing a subject with a light source in front of that person, you will usually get a reflection of that light in the eye, be it your flash, the sun, or something else brightly reflecting off the surface of the eye.

SETTING UP AND SHOOTING WITH FILL FLASH

1. Press the pop-up flash button to raise your pop-up flash into the ready position (**A**).

2. Press and hold the flash button while rotating the Sub-command dial until it reads -0.3 on the control panel (**B**).

3. Release the flash button.

4. Take a photograph and check your playback LCD to see if it looks good. If not, try reducing power in one-third-stop increments.

One problem that can quickly surface when using the on-camera flash is redeye. Not to worry, though—we will talk about how to remedy that in Chapter 8.

PORTRAITS ON THE MOVE

Not all portraits are shot with the subject sitting in a chair, posed and ready for the picture. Sometimes you might want to get an action shot that says something about the person, similar to an environmental portrait. Children, especially, just like to move. Why fight it? Set up an action portrait instead.

For the photo in **Figure 6.12**, I used the Portrait picture control and set my camera to Shutter Priority mode. I knew that there would be a good deal of movement involved, and I wanted to make sure that I had a fairly high shutter speed to freeze the action, so I set it to 1/320 of a second. I set the focus mode to AF-C and the drive mode to Continuous and just let it rip. There were quite a few throwaway shots, but I was able to capture one that conveyed the energy and action of the subject.

ISO 1600
1/320 sec.
f/11
18mm lens

FIGURE 6.12
A high ISO allowed me to use a fast shutter speed to stop the action, along with a small aperture to increase depth of field.

TIPS FOR SHOOTING BETTER PORTRAITS

Before we get to the assignments for this chapter, I thought it might be a good idea to leave you with a few extra pointers on shooting portraits, pointers that don't necessarily have anything specific to do with your camera. Entire books cover things like portrait lighting, posing, and so on. But here are a few simple tips that will make your people pics look a lot better.

IN GENERAL, AVOID THE CENTER OF THE FRAME

This falls under the category of composition. Instead of plunking your subject smack-dab in the middle for what I like to call the "mug shot" pose (**Figure 6.13**), position her toward the side of the frame (**Figure 6.14**)—it just looks more interesting.

On occasion, though, centering your subject works to your advantage in creating a mood. My best advice is to change it up and see which portrait conveys the message you're looking for, because there's no hard-and-fast rule, just options!

ISO 400
1/50 sec
f/4.5
35mm lens

FIGURE 6.13
This is what I call "the mug shot." It's when you frame your subject dead center against a solid surface or background with empty space on both sides. Notice how unhappy she looks (dramatized for effect!).

ISO 400
1/50 sec.
f/4.5
35mm lens

FIGURE 6.14
Create a more interesting portrait by placing your subject off to the side. Notice how happy she became when I improved my framing.

CHOOSE THE RIGHT LENS

Choosing the correct lens can make a huge impact on your portraits. A wide-angle lens can distort the features of your subject, which can lead to an unflattering portrait. I typically use a wide-angle lens only when I'm trying to capture more of the environment or when I'm photographing larger groups (**Figure 6.15**). Select a longer focal length for up-close and personal shots of the face. This helps fill the frame and reduce distortion (**Figure 6.16**).

ISO 200
1/400 sec.
f/2.8
35mm lens

FIGURE 6.15
At this close distance, I used a wide angle for a group portrait.

ISO 200
1/200 sec.
f/2.8
70mm lens

FIGURE 6.16
I centered the subject to create a serious mood and used a 70mm focal range to fill the frame.

USE THE FRAME

Have you ever noticed that most people are taller than they are wide? Turn your camera vertically for a more pleasing composition (**Figure 6.17**).

FIGURE 6.17
Get in the habit of turning your camera to a vertical position when shooting portraits. This is also referred to as portrait orientation.

ISO 125
1/80 sec.
f/7.1
70mm lens

FIGURE 6.18
An overcast sky
provided a soft,
even light source
for this picture
of traditionally
dressed girls in
Cusco, Peru. The
gentle light helped
soften their faces,
as well as bring out
the texture in their
colorful clothing.

ISO 250
1/250 sec.
f/2.8
48mm lens

SUNBLOCK FOR PORTRAITS

The midday sun can be harsh and can do unflattering things to people's faces.
If you can, find a shady spot out of the direct sunlight. You will get softer shadows,
smoother skin tones, and better detail. This holds true for overcast skies as well
(**Figure 6.18**). Just be sure to adjust your white balance accordingly.

GIVE THEM A HEALTHY GLOW

Nearly everyone looks better with a warm, healthy glow. Some of the best light of the
day happens just a little before sundown, so shoot at that time if you can (**Figure 6.19**).

FIGURE 6.19
You just can't beat
the glow of the late
afternoon sun for
adding warmth to
your portraits.

ISO 160
1/60 sec.
f/18
70mm lens

KEEP AN EYE ON YOUR BACKGROUND

Sometimes it's so easy to get caught up in taking a great shot that you forget about the smaller details. Try to keep an eye on what is going on behind your subjects so they don't end up with things popping out of their heads (**Figures 6.20** and **6.21**).

ISO 400
1/320 sec.
f/3.2
85mm lens

ISO 400
1/250 sec.
f/3.2
85mm lens

FIGURE 6.20
This photograph makes it appear that there is a pole going right through my daughter's head. It is important to slow down and notice these details.

FIGURE 6.21
By having her take just two steps to the left, I got the pole out of the scene entirely, making for a much-improved composition.

FRAME THE SCENE

Using elements in the scene to create a frame around your subject is a great way to draw the viewer in. You don't have to use a window frame to do this. Just look for elements in the foreground that could be employed to force the viewer's eye toward your subject (**Figure 6.22**).

MORE THAN JUST A PRETTY FACE

Most people think of a portrait as a photo of someone's face. Don't ignore other aspects of your subject that reflect his or her personality—hands, especially, can go a long way toward describing someone (**Figure 6.23**).

ISO 200
1/80 sec.
f/2.8
85mm lens

FIGURE 6.22
While these ladies were sitting in front of the fireplace to stay warm, I saw a perfect opportunity for a nice environmentally framed portrait. The bricks surrounding the fireplace created a natural frame for my subjects.

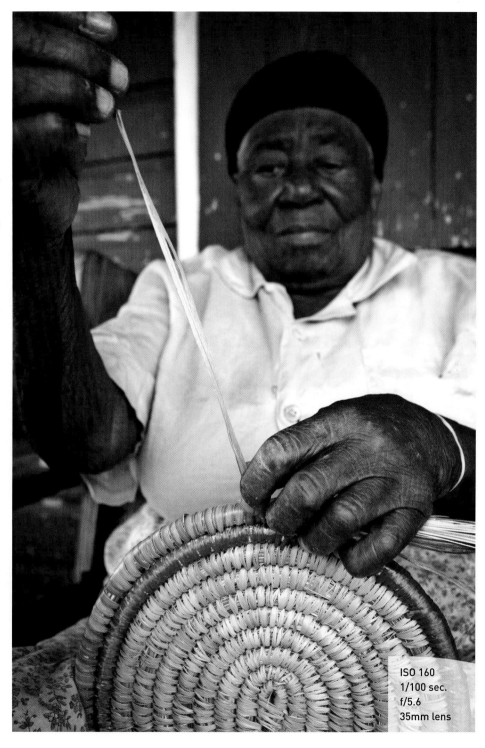

FIGURE 6.23

On Cat Island in the Bahamas, I drove up to this family's home because they were selling these beautiful baskets. I wanted to capture the entire scene, but I also wanted to show the weaver's hands. These hands had been making baskets for over 60 years, and I thought they told a story all by themselves.

ISO 160
1/100 sec.
f/5.6
35mm lens

GET DOWN ON THEIR LEVEL

If you want better pictures of children, don't shoot from an adult's eye level. Getting the camera down to the child's level will make your images look more personal (**Figure 6.24**).

ISO 100
1/400 sec.
f/9
65mm lens

FIGURE 6.24
While driving through rural Jamaica, we stopped at a school to get some photos. All the kids came running across the lot screaming with excitement. They loved having their photos taken as long as I kept showing them the playback images on the back of the camera.

ELIMINATE SPACE BETWEEN YOUR SUBJECTS

One of the problems you can encounter when taking portraits of more than one person is that of personal space. What feels like a close distance to the subjects can look impersonal to the viewer. Have your subjects move very close together, eliminating any open space between them (**Figure 6.25**).

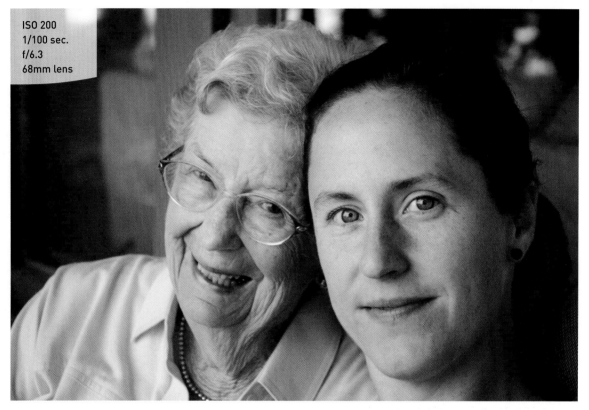

ISO 200
1/100 sec.
f/6.3
68mm lens

FIGURE 6.25
Getting your subjects close together tells a better story. At a family reunion I had my sister close to our 94-year-old grandmother to get this portrait, which captures their relationship.

Chapter 6 Assignments

Depth of field in portraits

Let's start with something simple. Grab someone you like and start experimenting with using different aperture settings. Shoot wide open (the widest your lens goes, such as f/2.8 or f/4) and then really stopped down (like f/22). Look at the difference in the depth of field and how it plays an important role in placing the attention on your subject. (Make sure you don't have your subject standing against the background. Get some distance so that there is a good blurring effect of the background at the wide f-stop setting.)

Discovering the qualities of natural light

Pick a nice sunny day and try shooting some portraits in the midday sun. If your subject is willing, have him turn so the sun is in his face. If he is still speaking to you after you blinded him, have him turn his back to the sun. Try this with and without the fill flash so you can see the difference. Finally, move him into a completely shaded spot and take a few more.

Picking the right metering method

Find a very dark or light background and place your subject in front of it. Now take a couple of shots, allowing a lot of space around your subject for the background to show. Now switch metering modes and use the AE Lock feature to get a more accurate reading of your subject. Notice the differences in exposure between the metering methods.

Approach a stranger and practice your street photography. Find a busy, public place and ask someone if you can take her picture. If she declines, find someone else. Remember to smile and act comfortable. Offer her your business card or e-mail address so she can e-mail you to get the portrait. Then, practice taking some shots using some environmental data to tell a story.

If this is the first time you've done this, it's natural to be nervous. Just remember that it becomes easier with practice.

Share your results with the book's Flickr group!
Join the group here: flickr.com/groups/nikond7100_fromsnapshotstogreatshots.

7

ISO 100
1/400 sec.
f/9
15mm lens

Landscape Photography

TIPS, TOOLS, AND TECHNIQUES FOR TAKING BEAUTIFUL LANDSCAPE PHOTOGRAPHS

I grew up in northern Michigan and spent most of my life enjoying the wilderness with my friends and family. On Sundays it was a tradition to load up the station wagon and go for a drive in the countryside. When I wasn't picking on my sister I could be found staring out the backseat window, drifting in and out of conscious thought and dreaming of places I wanted to see. Now, some 30 years later, I find myself still drawn to visiting many of nature's true wonders—this time with camera in tow.

In this chapter, we will explore some typical scenarios and discuss methods to bring out the best in your landscape photography. We'll delve into some of the features of the D7100 that not only improve the look of your landscape photography, but also make it easier to take great shots.

PORING OVER THE PICTURE

I lead an annual landscape photography workshop in Death Valley, and each year I try to approach things a little differently. I've photographed Zabriskie Point several times and normally tackle the image with a wide-angle lens. However, this last time I decided to experiment with a little trick called lens compression. This technique makes things look closer to us than they really are, as well as making objects in the frame appear closer to one another than they really are. To achieve this effect you need to use a zoom lens, and for this particular shot a focal length of 100mm seemed to do the trick. Lens compression allowed me to bring attention to the interesting rock formations by flattening the rolling hills and creating a visual illusion of layers.

Using a neutral density filter, I was able to expose the foreground correctly without losing detail.

ISO 100
1/30 sec.
f/8
100mm lens

When it comes to popular sites like Zabriskie Point, you'd better be ready to be on site an hour before daylight to beat the droves of fellow photographers.

I bracketed the shot using three exposures so that I could later create an HDR (high dynamic range) image.

I zoomed to a focal length of 100mm to take advantage of lens compression, creating the illusion of layers.

SHARP FOCUS: USING A TRIPOD

Throughout the previous chapters we have concentrated on using the camera to create great images. We will continue that focus through this chapter, but we'll add into the mix a piece of equipment that is crucial in the world of landscape shooting: the tripod. There are a couple of reasons tripods are so critical to your landscape work, the first being the time of day that you will be working. As we'll cover later, the best light for most landscape work happens at sunrise and just before sunset. While this is the best time to shoot, it's also kind of dark. That means you'll be working with slow shutter speeds. Slow shutter speeds mean camera shake, unless you take precautions. Camera shake equals bad photos.

The second reason is also related to the amount of light that you're gathering with your camera. When taking landscape photos, you will usually want to be working with very small apertures, as they give you lots of depth of field. This also means that, once again, you will be working with slower-than-normal shutter speeds.

Slow shutter = camera shake = blurry photos.

If you're serious about landscape photography, then the one tool that you must have is a good tripod. We might argue over what camera or what lens, but we all agree a tripod is key to getting a good image (**Figure 7.1**). The story behind Figure 7.1 is that while I thought I was going to beat everyone to the punch and get this shot at just

FIGURE 7.1
All of these photographers are using tripods at the Moulton Barn in Wyoming. You will also notice that it was a low-light situation, taking place as soon as the sun came up.

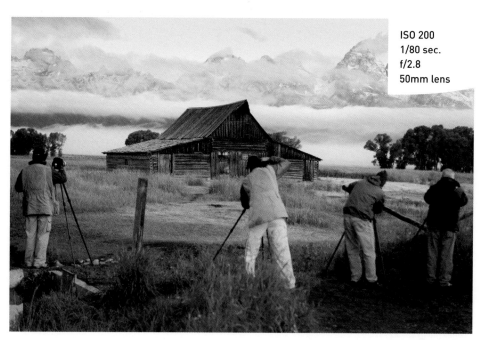

ISO 200
1/80 sec.
f/2.8
50mm lens

the right time, apparently they had figured this out well before I did, and I hadn't set my alarm quite early enough. I lost my place to four other photographers, who had done a little more research. I learned my lesson and it's never happened since!

So what should you look for in a tripod? Well, first make sure it is sturdy enough to support your camera and any lens that you might want to use. Most manufacturers will list the weight limits by model. Next, check the height of the tripod. There is nothing worse than having to bend over all day to look through your viewfinder. Think about getting a tripod that uses a quick-release head. This usually employs a plate that screws into the bottom of the camera and then quickly snaps into place on the tripod. A quick-release head is especially handy if you are going to move between shooting by hand and using the tripod. Finally, consider the weight of the tripod. If you're traveling a lot or backpacking, having a heavy tripod is a real burden. Carbon-fiber tripods are nice because they are very light and incredibly sturdy, but of course that combination comes at an increased cost.

Manual Callout

Another way to reduce camera shake is to use Mirror-up mode with a cable release or remote. Simply press the Release Mode dial lock and turn the Release Mode dial to MUP. Make sure to frame your image, set your exposure, and set your focus before you press the cable release button. Once you're happy with the image, press the release and the camera will raise the mirror. Then, simply press the cable release button one more time to take the picture. For more on Mirror-up mode, please review page 61 of your manual.

VR LENSES AND TRIPODS DON'T MIX

If you are using Vibration Reduction (VR) lenses on your camera, you need to remember to turn this feature off when you use a tripod. This is because Vibration Reduction can, while trying to minimize camera movement, actually create movement when the camera is already stable. To turn off the VR feature, just slide the VR selector switch on the side of the lens to the Off position (**Figure 7.2**).

FIGURE 7.2
Turn off the Vibration Reduction feature when using a tripod.

SELECTING THE PROPER ISO

When you are shooting most landscape scenes, the ISO is the one factor that should be increased only as a last resort. While it is easy to select a higher ISO to get a smaller aperture, the noise that it can introduce into your images can be quite harmful. The noise is not only visible as large grainy artifacts, it can also be multicolored, which further degrades the image quality.

When shooting landscapes, set your ISO to the lowest possible setting at all times (**Figure 7.3**). Between the use of Vibration Reduction lenses (if you are shooting handheld) and a good tripod, you will seldom need to shoot landscapes with anything above an ISO of 400.

ISO 200
1/320 sec.
f/7.1
35mm lens

FIGURE 7.3
I used a very low ISO of 200 in order to maintain the best image quality possible given the available light.

USING NOISE REDUCTION

The temptation to use higher ISOs should always be avoided, because it will result in more image noise and less detail. Even when you have your camera set to a low ISO, however, noise can be introduced when the shutter is held open for too long during a long exposure. Long exposures are fun to take but are notorious for introducing noise in an image. This noise is the result of the heating of the camera sensor while in use. The longer the exposure, the longer the sensor works and heats up, creating "hot pixels," or noise. This effect is not visible in short exposures, but as you start shooting with shutter speeds that exceed one second, the level of image noise can increase. Your camera has a built-in Noise Reduction (NR) feature to help eliminate noise from long exposures. The camera reduces noise by taking two images, the original exposure followed by another exposure with the shutter closed. The camera then measures the "hot pixels" created by the heating of the sensor and subtracts the noise pattern from the original exposure. The downside to this technique is that it doubles your exposure time, so be prepared to wait while the camera does its job.

SETTING UP LONG EXPOSURE NOISE REDUCTION

1. Press the Menu button, then use the Multi-selector to select Long Exposure NR from the Shooting menu (**A**).

2. While Long Exposure NR is highlighted, press the OK button. Next, move the Multi-selector up to select On. Press the OK button to activate (**B**).

3. While the goal is to always use as low an ISO as possible, at times you may have to use a higher ISO. For instance, available light might be dwindling with no tripod in sight, so we need to increase our ISO so that we can handhold our camera without introducing camera shake. The D7100 has really upped its game from its predecessor in this area, and you may even find yourself shooting at ISO 1600 without any visible noise. But you still might come across some

shooting situations when noise is very apparent as a result of the higher ISO. To combat noise at higher ISOs, the D7100 has a High ISO Noise Reduction feature that basically blurs the image in camera to reduce the visible noise. I suggest using this feature only when you have visible noise in your image and don't plan on using noise reduction software in post-processing.

ACTIVATING HIGH ISO NOISE REDUCTION

1. Press the Menu button, then use the Multi-selector to select High ISO from the Shooting menu and press OK (**A**).

2. Now use the Multi-selector to choose from one of four options: High, Normal, Low, and Off. Select one and press OK to activate (**B**). Be aware, ISO Noise Reduction can be activated only when your ISO exceeds 1200.

3. I suggest experimenting with different ISOs and NR settings to establish ones that meet your expectations.

A

B

SELECTING A WHITE BALANCE

This probably seems like a no-brainer. If it's sunny, select Daylight. If it's overcast, choose the Shade or Cloudy setting. Those choices wouldn't be wrong for those circumstances, but why not get creative? Sometimes you can actually make the mood of the photo more intriguing by selecting a white balance that doesn't quite fit the light for the scene that you are shooting.

Figure 7.4 is an example of a correct white balance. It was late afternoon and the sun was starting to move low in the sky, giving everything that warm afternoon glow. The white balance for this image was set to Daylight.

But what if I want to make the scene look like it was shot in the early morning hours? Simple—I just change the white balance to Fluorescent, which is a much cooler setting (**Figure 7.5**).

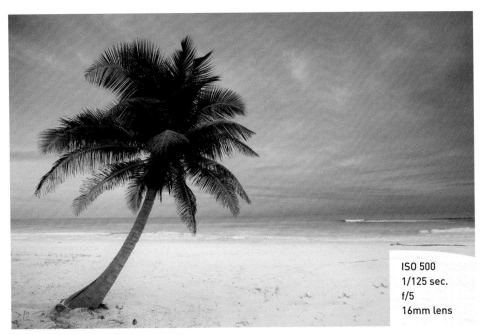

ISO 500
1/125 sec.
f/5
16mm lens

FIGURE 7.4
Using the correct white balance produces an appealing image.

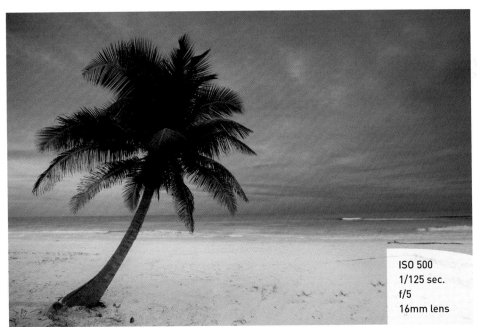

ISO 500
1/125 sec.
f/5
16mm lens

FIGURE 7.5
Changing the white balance to Fluorescent gives the image a totally different look and feel without the need to go into post-production software to change the look.

You can select the most appropriate white balance for your shooting conditions in a couple of ways. The first is to just take a shot, review it on the LCD, and keep the one you like. Of course, you would need to take one for each white balance setting, which means that you would have to take about seven different shots to see which was most pleasing.

The second method doesn't require taking a single shot. Instead, it uses Live View to get perfectly selected white balances. Live View gives instant feedback as you scroll through all of the White Balance settings and displays them for you right on the LCD. Even better, you can choose a custom setting that will let you dial in exactly the right look for your image.

To use Live View to preview the white balance, first you need to turn Live View on by pressing the LV button. Next, hold the WB button, as discussed in Chapter 1, while rotating the main Command dial to the right (**Figure 7.6**).

FIGURE 7.6
Press the LV button to get instant feedback on all your White Balance options. You can even choose a custom setting.

Finally, for those of you who might like creating your own custom white balances, the D7100 has introduced a new feature that allows you to spot white balance and create six custom presets while using Live View.

SPOT WHITE BALANCE IN LIVE VIEW

1. To set your custom white balance, press the LV button to activate Live View.

2. Next, press the WB button while rotating the main Command dial until PRE1 is displayed in the top right corner. Release the WB button.*

3. Now, press the WB button until the PRE icon begins to flash. Once it's flashing, a yellow square balance target will appear in the middle of the Live View screen.

4. Place the spot white balance target over a neutral color area, such as a gray or white. Next, press the OK button. If the spot white balance target was recorded correctly, then the words Data Acquired will be displayed on the LCD.

5. Your custom presets may also be accessed via the Shooting menu.

6. Press Menu and then select White Balance with your Multi-selector (**A**).

7. Press the OK button, then move the Multi-selector to the right to display all six presets. The presets will provide a visual confirmation of where the spot balance target was placed on the image to generate the custom white balance (**B**).

*In the future, you will be able to record and access up to six custom presets by following the previous steps. However, at step three you would want to use the Sub-command dial to access the other five presets.

USING THE LANDSCAPE PICTURE CONTROL

When shooting landscapes, I always look for great color and contrast. These qualities are two of the reasons that so many landscape shots are taken in the early morning or during sunset. When the sun is at a low angle, it creates a softer light, which adds more texture and richer colors to any scene. That's why we call it the golden hour. You can help boost this effect, especially in the less-than-golden hours of the day, by using the Landscape picture control (**Figure 7.7**). Just as in the Landscape mode found in the automatic scene modes, you can set up your landscape shooting so that you capture images with increased sharpness and a slight boost in blues and greens. This style will add some pop to your landscapes without the need for additional processing in any software.

> Manual Callout
>
> Check out page 105 in your camera manual for more information on setting picture controls.

ISO 125
1/320 sec.
f/14
16mm lens

FIGURE 7.7
Using the Landscape picture control can add sharpness and more vivid color to skies and vegetation. Here it helped me capture the orange and turquoise colors that make the Grand Prismatic Spring so amazing.

SETTING UP THE LANDSCAPE PICTURE CONTROL

1. Press the *i* button, then use the Multi-selector to highlight the Set Picture Control feature (this is normally set to SD) and then press OK (**A**).

2. Now use the Multi-selector to scroll down to the LS option and press OK to lock in your change (**B**).

The camera will now apply the Landscape picture control to all of your photos. This style will be locked in to the camera even after turning it off and back on again, so make sure to change it back to SD when you are done with your landscape shoot.

TAMING BRIGHT SKIES WITH EXPOSURE COMPENSATION

Balancing exposure in scenes that have a wide contrast in tonal ranges can be extremely challenging. The one thing you should never do is overexpose your skies to the point of blowing out your highlights (unless, of course, that is the look you are going for). It's one thing to have white clouds, but it's a completely different, and bad, thing to have no detail at all in those clouds. This usually happens when the camera is trying to gain exposure in the darker areas of the image (**Figure 7.8**).

With the Exposure Compensation feature, you can force your camera to choose an exposure that ranges, in one-third-stop increments, from five stops over to five stops under the metered exposure (**Figure 7.9**).

The one way to tell if you have blown out your highlights is to turn on the Highlight Alert, often referred to as the "blinkies," feature on your camera (see the "How I Shoot: My Favorite Camera Settings" section in Chapter 4). When you take a shot where the highlights are exposed beyond the point of having any detail, that area will blink in your LCD. It is up to you to determine if that particular area is important enough to regain detail by altering your exposure. If the answer is yes, then the easiest way to go about it is to use some exposure compensation.

ISO 800
1/200 sec.
f/11
24mm lens

ISO 800
1/1000 sec.
f/11
24mm lens

FIGURE 7.8
The sand and the grass are well exposed, but the sky is totally blown out. Whenever I'm shooting into a sunset, this is a potential problem. I solve it by using Exposure Compensation to get the entire image exposed correctly.

FIGURE 7.9
I compensated my exposure by two stops (-2 on the Exposure Compensation adjustment) and was able to bring details back into the clouds, sky, and water. You will notice the image itself is darker as a result of this compensation.

USING EXPOSURE COMPENSATION TO REGAIN DETAIL IN HIGHLIGHTS

1. Activate the camera meter by lightly pressing the shutter release button.

2. Using your index finger, press and hold the Exposure Compensation button to change the over-/underexposure setting by rotating the main Command dial.

3. Rotate the main Command dial to the left one click and take another picture (each click of the dial is a one-third-stop change).

4. If the blinkies are gone, you are good to go. If not, keep subtracting from your exposure by one-third of a stop until you have a good exposure in the highlights.

ADJUSTING EXPOSURE COMPENSATION

1. Press the Exposure Compensation button (which has a +/- symbol on it) on the top of the camera to adjust exposure by -5 to +5 stops.

2. Hold the Exposure Compensation button while rotating the main Command dial to the left to increase exposure and to the right to decrease exposure. Each right click of the dial will continue to reduce the exposure in one-third-stop increments for up to five stops (although I rarely need to go past two stops).

It should be noted that any exposure compensation will remain in place even after turning the camera off and then on again. Don't forget to reset it once you have successfully captured your image. Also, the Exposure Compensation feature works only in the Program, Shutter Priority, Aperture Priority, and Manual modes. Changing between these four modes will hold the compensation you set while switching from one to the other. When you change the Mode dial to one of the automatic scene modes, the compensation will set itself to zero.

SHOOTING AMAZING BLACK-AND-WHITE LANDSCAPES

There is almost nothing as timeless as a beautiful black-and-white landscape photo. For many, it is the purest form of photography. The genre conjures up thoughts of Ansel Adams out in Yosemite Valley, capturing stunning monoliths with his 8 x 10 view camera. Shooting with a digital camera doesn't mean you can't create your own stunning photos, using the power of the Monochrome picture control. (See the "Classic Black-and-White Portraits" section of Chapter 6 for instructions on setting up this feature.) Not only can you shoot in black and white, you can also customize the camera to apply built-in filters to lighten or darken elements within your scene, as well as add contrast and definition.

The four filter colors are red, yellow, green, and orange. The most typically used filters in black-and-white photography are red and yellow. This is because the color of these filters will darken opposite colors and lighten similar colors. So if you want to darken a blue sky, use a yellow filter because blue is the opposite of yellow. To darken green foliage, you would use a red filter. Check out the shot in **Figure 7.10** with a red filter applied.

You can see that there is no real difference in contrast between the color and the black-and-white image with no filter. A red filter effect can help create contrast by darkening the sky and making the green foliage much darker. Other options in the Monochrome picture control enable you to adjust the sharpness and contrast and even add some color toning to the final image. This information is also in the "Classic Black-and-White Portraits" section of Chapter 6. Experiment with the various settings to find the combination that is most pleasing to you.

ISO 125
1/125 sec.
f/8
16mm lens

FIGURE 7.10
In the first shot, taken in color, notice the bright blue skies and green grass. The second shot was done with the Monochrome setting. The third image was shot with a red filter applied in the Monochrome setting with contrast increased. Adding color filter settings to the Monochrome picture control allows you to lighten or darken elements in your scene.

THE GOLDEN LIGHT

If you ask any professional landscape photographer what his or her favorite time of day to shoot is, chances are the photographer will tell you it's the hours surrounding daybreak and sunset (**Figure 7.11**). The reason for this is that the light is coming from a very low angle to the landscape, which creates shadows and gives depth and character. There is also a quality to the light that seems cleaner and is more colorful than what you get when shooting at midday. One thing that can dramatically improve any morning or evening shot is the presence of clouds. The sun will fill the underside of the clouds with a palette of colors and add drama to your skies.

FIGURE 7.11
The last few minutes of light after the sun has set is probably one of my favorite moments to capture images.

WARM AND COOL COLOR TEMPERATURES

These two terms are used to describe the overall colorcast of an image. Reds and yellows are said to be *warm*, which is usually the look that you get from the late afternoon sun. Blue is normally the predominant color when talking about a *cool* cast.

ISO 100
8 sec.
f/11
35mm lens

WHERE TO PLACE YOUR FOCUS

Large landscape scenes are great fun to photograph, but they can present a problem: Where exactly do you focus when you want everything to be sharp? Since our goal is to create a great landscape photo, we will need to concentrate on how to best create an image that is tack sharp, with a depth of field that renders great focus throughout the scene.

I have already stressed the importance of a good tripod when shooting landscapes. The tripod lets you concentrate on the aperture portion of the exposure without worrying how long your shutter will be open. This is because the tripod provides the stability to handle any shutter speed you might need when shooting at small apertures. I find that for most of my landscape work I set my camera to Aperture Priority mode, with the ISO set to 100 (for a clean, noise-free image).

However, shooting with the smallest aperture on your lens doesn't necessarily mean that you will get the proper sharpness throughout your image. The real key is knowing where in the scene to focus your lens to maximize the depth of field for your chosen aperture. To determine this, you must use something called the hyper focal distance of your lens.

Hyper focal distance, also referred to as HFD, is the point of focus that will give you the greatest acceptable sharpness from a point near your camera all the way out to infinity. If you combine good HFD practice with a small aperture, you will get images that are sharp to infinity.

A couple of ways exist to do this, and the one that is probably the easiest, as you might guess, is the one that is most widely used by working pros. When you have your shot all set up and composed, focus on an object that is about one-third of the distance into your frame (**Figure 7.12**). It is usually pretty close to the proper distance and will render favorable results. When you have the focus set, take a photograph and then zoom in on the preview on your LCD to check the sharpness of your image.

One thing to remember is that as your lens gets wider in focal length, your HFD will be closer to the camera position. This is because the wider the lens, the greater the depth of field you can achieve. This is yet another reason why a good wide-angle lens is indispensable to the landscape shooter.

ISO 100
1/60 sec.
f/16
12mm lens

FIGURE 7.12

To get maximum focus from near to far, I manually focused one-third of the way into the frame, or at the beginning of the building structures. I then recomposed the image before taking the picture. Using AF-S focus mode and f/16 gave me a very sharp image throughout the frame.

FOCUSING WITH LIVE VIEW

There's no denying that the automatic focus features on the D7100 are great, but sometimes it pays to turn them off and go manual. The reason I use manual focus is to avoid having the camera's autofocus inadvertently refocus when the shutter is released. I always start out with the assistance of autofocus but then switch over to manual focus to avoid any refocusing mistakes. Then I like to take it a step further and cheat a bit by using Live View along with the Playback Zoom In button to assure absolute sharpness throughout the image (**Figure 7.13**).

IMPROVING YOUR FOCUS USING LIVE VIEW

1. Compose your shot either using the viewfinder or activating Live View by pressing the LV button (**A**).

2. Set your camera to AF-S mode and use one of the 51 focus points to select the area you wish to focus on. Remember, you can use your Multi-selector to move around. Next, press the shutter button halfway to focus the camera.

3. Switch the camera to manual focus by sliding the switch on the lens barrel from A to M and turn off VR (if your lens comes equipped with Vibration Reduction) (**B**).

4. With Live View activated, use the Zoom In button with the aid of the Multi-selector to pan the image for sharpness. If it's blurry, then make small adjustments with your lens focus ring until ideal sharpness is achieved. Now take the shot using a cable release, remote, or self-timer feature.

A

B

The camera will fire without trying to refocus the lens. This works especially well for wide-angle lenses, which can be difficult to focus in manual mode.

ISO 125
1/320 sec.
f/4
35mm lens

FIGURE 7.13
I used the rule of thirds (discussed later in the chapter) to help frame this image by placing the purple tulip at the point where the vertical and horizontal lines intersect. Using Live View with manual focus allowed me to make sure the purple tulip was tack sharp while blurring the background.

SMOOTH WATER

There's little that is quite as satisfying for the landscape shooter as capturing a smooth waterfall shot. Creating the smooth-flowing effect is as simple as adjusting your shutter speed to allow the water to be in motion while the shutter is open. The key is to have your camera on a stable platform (such as a tripod) so that you can use a shutter speed that's long enough to work (**Figure 7.14**). To achieve a great effect, use a shutter speed that is at least 1/15 of a second or longer.

FIGURE 7.14
I sat my tripod right in the middle of this creek downstream from these small rapids. This allowed me to get the right point of view while using a slow shutter speed to show the movement in the water.

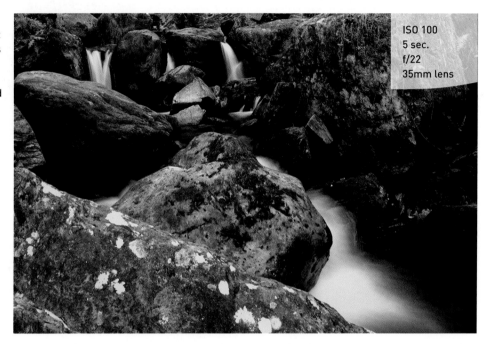

ISO 100
5 sec.
f/22
35mm lens

SETTING UP FOR A WATERFALL SHOT

1. Attach the camera to your tripod, then compose and focus your shot.
2. Make sure the ISO is set to 100.
3. Using Aperture Priority mode, set your aperture to the smallest opening (such as f/22 or f/36).
4. Press the shutter button halfway so the camera takes a meter reading.
5. Check to see if the shutter speed is 1/15 or slower.
6. Take a photo and then check the image on the LCD.

You can also use Shutter Priority mode for this effect by dialing in the desired shutter speed and having the camera set the aperture for you. I prefer to use Aperture Priority to ensure that I have the greatest depth of field possible.

If the water is blinking on the LCD, indicating a loss of detail in the highlights, then use the Exposure Compensation feature (as discussed earlier in this chapter) to bring details back into the water. You will need to have the Highlight Alert feature turned on to check for overexposure (see "How I Shoot: My Favorite Camera Settings" in Chapter 4).

It is possible that you won't get a shutter speed that is long enough to capture a smooth effect, especially if you are shooting in bright conditions. To overcome this obstacle, you need a lens filter—either a polarizing filter or a neutral density filter.

The polarizing filter redirects wavelengths of light to create more vibrant colors, reduce reflections, and darken blue skies, as well as lengthen exposure times by two stops due to the darkness of the filter. It is a handy filter for landscape work. The neutral density filter is typically just a dark piece of glass that serves to darken the scene by one, two, or three stops. This allows you to use slower shutter speeds during bright conditions. Think of it as sunglasses for your camera lens.

DIRECTING THE VIEWER'S EYE: A WORD ABOUT COMPOSITION

As a photographer, it's your job to lead the viewer through your image. You accomplish this by using the principles of composition, which is the arrangement of elements in the scene that draws the viewer's eyes through your image and holds that person's attention. You need to understand how people see and then use that information to focus their attention on the most important elements in your image.

There is a general order in which we look at elements in a photograph. The first is brightness. The eye wants to travel to the brightest object in a scene. So if you have a bright sky, it's the first place the eye will go. The second is sharpness. Sharp, detailed elements get more attention than soft, blurry areas. Finally, the eye will move first to vivid colors and last to dull, flat colors to grab, keep, and then direct the viewer's attention through the frame.

In **Figure 7.15**, the eye is drawn to the bright splashes of water and the sharply focused rocks in the foreground. From there it is pulled up the river, where the frame gets darker and the eye comes to rest on the mountains and the shore. Finally, the viewer's gaze moves up into the active sky, starting with the light fluffy clouds and ending in the dark blue at the very top of the frame.

FIGURE 7.15

I enjoy fly-fishing the Madison River in Montana so much that I decided to photograph my favorite trout stream. Standing in the water with my waders on, I took this shot of the river. When composing, it I wanted the viewer's eye to be drawn into the image and pulled up to the mountains and the wispy clouds above.

ISO 200
1/500 sec.
f/10
16mm lens

ISO 125
1/60 sec.
f/13
16mm lens

FIGURE 7.16
I wanted to show
all the dead trees
in this paint pot
at Yellowstone
National Park, so I
decided to compose
the image with the
nearest tree in the
bottom right quad-
rant. This created
a more compelling
composition than
centering the tree.

RULE OF THIRDS

There are quite a few philosophies concerning composition. The easiest to begin with is the rule of thirds. Using this principle, you simply divide your viewfinder into thirds by imagining two horizontal and two vertical lines that divide the frame equally.

The key to using this method of composition is to have your main subject located at or near one of the intersecting points (**Figure 7.16**).

By placing your subject near these intersecting lines, you give the viewer space to move within the frame. The one thing you normally don't want to do is center your subject in the frame, sometimes called "bull's-eye" composition. Centering the subject is not always wrong, but will usually be less appealing and may not hold the viewer's attention.

Another rule of thirds deals with horizon lines. Generally, you should position the horizon one-third of the way up or down in the frame. Splitting the frame by placing your horizon in the middle is akin to placing the subject in the middle of the frame; it doesn't lend a sense of importance to either the sky or the ground.

In **Figure 7.17**, I used the rule of thirds by aligning my horizon in the bottom third of the frame and the sky and steam in the top third. I placed the river in the foreground to draw the eye to the bottom third of the frame, letting the viewer travel throughout the frame, ending on the steam, sky, and bright sun. The top two-thirds contain the sky and the steam rising from the geothermal features in Yellowstone National Park.

FIGURE 7.17
Putting the horizon of this image at the bottom third of the frame places emphasis on steam rising from the geo-thermal features in the landscape.

ISO 200
1/100 sec.
f/22
24mm lens

The D7100 has a visual tool for assisting you in composing your photo in the form of grid overlay. This grid can be set to appear in the viewfinder and on the rear LCD when you are in Live View mode.

USING A GRID OVERLAY IN THE VIEWFINDER

1. Press the Menu button, then use the Multi-selector to navigate to the Custom Settings menu and select D Shooting/Display.

2. Navigate to D2 Viewfinder Grid Display (**A**) and press OK.

3. Move the Multi-selector up to highlight On and press OK (**B**).

A

B

USING A GRID OVERLAY IN LIVE VIEW

1. Press the Live View button to turn on Live View.

2. Press the Info button until the grid appears on the viewfinder.

Although the grid in the viewfinder and the Live View screen aren't equally divided into thirds, they will give you an approximation of where you should be aligning your subjects in the frame.

CREATING DEPTH

Because a photograph is a flat, two-dimensional space, you need to establish a sense of depth by using the elements in the scene to create a three-dimensional feel. This is accomplished by including different and distinct spaces for the eye to travel to: a foreground, a middle ground, and a background. By using these three spaces, you draw the viewer in and give your image depth.

The image in **Figure 7.18** was taken in my hometown on one of my favorite country roads. I'm a country boy at heart, and I spent countless hours of my late adolescence four-wheeling down this road with one goal in mind: getting my truck dirty! Now, years later, I find myself drawn to this scene because of the classic vanishing points surrounded by tall maple trees. This scene pulls me in as I find myself wandering down the road.

A vanishing point is one example of how you can create depth and draw a viewer into an image. I composed the image by adding a bit of dramatic light, splitting the sun in the arch of a tree and creating a sunburst effect by using a higher f-stop (f/16 in this case, although it could be higher in others). All of these factors helped give the image depth and made it feel three-dimensional.

ISO 125
.8 sec.
f/16
24mm lens

FIGURE 7.18
I like using classic vanishing points in my photography because they create a sense of depth, and in some cases a feeling of tranquility, as in this image.

ADVANCED TECHNIQUES TO EXPLORE

This section comes with a warning attached. All of the techniques and topics up to this point have been centered on your camera and hardware like tripods. The following two sections, covering panoramas and high dynamic range (HDR) images, require you to use image-processing software to complete the photograph. These two popular techniques are, however, important enough that you should know how to shoot for success should you choose to explore them.

SHOOTING PANORAMAS

I was never much for panoramas until I visited the Grand Teton National Park. The Tetons are probably one of my favorite mountain ranges and easily identifiable, but a single frame just doesn't do them justice. Only a panorama can truly capture a mountain range, cityscape, or any extremely wide vista.

ISO 100
1/250 sec.
f/8
80mm lens

THE MULTIPLE-IMAGE PANORAMA

To shoot a true panorama, you need to use either a special panorama camera that shoots a very wide frame or the following method, which requires the combining of multiple frames.

The multiple-image pano, as photographers often call a panoramic, has gained in popularity in the past few years; this is principally due to advances in image-processing software. Many software options available now will take multiple images, align them, and then "stitch" them into a single panoramic image. The real key to shooting a multiple-image pano is to overlap your shots by about 30 percent from one frame to the next (**Figures 7.19** and **7.20**). It is possible to handhold the camera while capturing your images, but the best method for capturing great panoramic images is to use a tripod.

Now that you have your series of overlapping images, you can import them into your image-processing software to stitch them together and create a single panoramic image.

FIGURE 7.19
Here you see the makings of a panorama, with nine shots overlapping by about 30 percent from frame to frame.

FIGURE 7.20
I used Adobe Photoshop to combine all of the exposures into one large panoramic image.

SORTING YOUR SHOTS FOR THE MULTI-IMAGE PANORAMA

If you shoot more than one series of shots for your panoramas, it can sometimes be difficult to know when the first series of images ends and the next begins. Here is a quick tip for separating your images.

Set up your camera using the steps listed below. Now, before you take your first good exposure in the series, hold up one finger in front of the camera and take a shot. Move your hand away and begin taking your overlapping images. When you have taken your last shot, hold two fingers in front of the camera and take another shot.

Now, when you go to review your images, use the series of shots that falls between the frames with one and two fingers in them. Then just repeat the process for your next panorama series.

SHOOTING PROPERLY FOR A MULTIPLE-IMAGE PANORAMA

1. Mount your camera on your tripod and make sure it is level.*

2. In Aperture Priority mode, use a very small aperture for the greatest depth of field. Take a meter reading of a bright part of the scene, and make note of aperture and shutter speed.

3. Now change your camera to Manual mode (M), and dial in the aperture and shutter speed that you obtained in the previous step.

4. Set your lens to manual focus, and then focus it for the area of interest using the HFD method of finding a point one-third of the way into the scene. (If you use the autofocus, you risk getting different points of focus from image to image, which will make the image stitching more difficult for the software.)

5. While carefully panning your camera, shoot your images to cover the entire area of the scene from one end to the other, leaving a 30 percent overlap from one frame to the next. The final step involves using your favorite imaging software, such as Photoshop, to take all of the photographs and combine them into a single panoramic image.

*HOT TIP

Use your camera's built-in level by activating LV and pressing the Info button several times until the camera level tool is displayed. This feature enables you to establish horizontal level by moving the camera until a green line appears to indicate that it is level.

SHOOTING HIGH DYNAMIC RANGE (HDR) IMAGES

High dynamic range (HDR) can create stunning images by using the full tonal range of an image, especially when recorded as a RAW file. Depending upon your preference, HDR images can look quite real or very surreal. I have found people either love or hate HDR, but regardless of what side of the fence you are on, it is a wonderful way to understand the effects of exposure on an image.

HDR is used quite often in landscape, cityscape, and, believe it or not, interior design images. Typically, when you photograph a scene that has a wide range of tones from shadows to highlights, you have to make a decision regarding which tonal values you are going to emphasize, and then adjust your exposure accordingly. This is because your camera has a limited dynamic range, at least as compared to the human eye. HDR photography allows you to capture multiple exposures for the highlights, shadows, and midtones, and then combine them into a single image using software (**Figure 7.21**).

ISO 125
1/160 sec.
f/20
16mm lens

FIGURE 7.21
This HDR image combines several exposures combined in HDR Efex Pro 2 and converted to black and white.

A number of software applications allow you to combine images and then merge them into a single HDR image. I will not be covering the software applications, but I will explore the process of shooting a scene to help you render properly captured images for the HDR process. Note that using a tripod is essential for this technique, since you need to have perfect alignment of the images when they are combined.

SETTING UP FOR SHOOTING AN HDR IMAGE

1. Set your ISO to 100 to ensure clean, noise-free images.

2. Set your program mode to Aperture Priority. During the shooting process, you will be taking three shots of the same scene, creating an overexposed image, an underexposed image, and a normal exposure. Since the camera is going to be adjusting the exposure, you want it to make changes to the shutter speed, not the aperture, so that your depth of field is consistent.

3. Set your camera file format to RAW. This is extremely important because the RAW format contains a much larger range of exposure values than a JPEG file, and the HDR software needs this information.

4. Change your shooting mode to Continuous Drive mode. This will allow you to capture your exposures quickly. Even though you will be using a tripod, there is always a chance that something within your scene will be moving (like clouds or leaves). Shooting in the Continuous mode minimizes any subject movement between frames.

5. Adjust the Auto Bracketing (BKT) mode to shoot three exposures in two-stop increments. To do this, you will first need to press the BKT button while moving the main Command dial to the right.

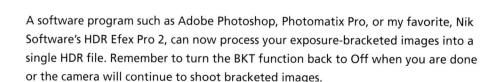

6. Now use the Sub-command dial to adjust the bracketing to 2.0.

7. Focus the camera using the manual focus method discussed earlier in the chapter, compose your shot, secure the tripod, and hold down the shutter button until the camera has fired three consecutive times. The result will be one normal exposure, as well as one under- and one overexposed image.

A software program such as Adobe Photoshop, Photomatix Pro, or my favorite, Nik Software's HDR Efex Pro 2, can now process your exposure-bracketed images into a single HDR file. Remember to turn the BKT function back to Off when you are done or the camera will continue to shoot bracketed images.

BRACKETING YOUR EXPOSURES

In HDR, *bracketing* is the process of capturing a series of exposures at different stop intervals. You can bracket your exposures even if you aren't going to be using HDR. Sometimes this is helpful when you have a tricky lighting situation and you want to ensure that you have just the right exposure to capture the look you're after. In HDR, you bracket to the plus and minus side of a "normal" exposure, but you can also bracket all of your exposures to the over or under side of normal. It all depends on what you are after. If you aren't sure whether you are getting enough shadow detail, you can bracket a little toward the overexposed side. The same is true for highlights. You can bracket in increments as small as a third of a stop.

This means that you can capture several images with very subtle exposure variances and then decide later which one is best. If you want to bracket just to one side of a normal exposure, set your exposure compensation to +1 or –1, whichever way you need, and then use the bracketing feature to automatically bracket your exposures.

USING YOUR CAMERA'S BUILT-IN HDR FEATURE

When the D7100 was released, I was really excited to hear that Nikon had introduced an HDR feature in the camera, but upon examination of it, I've concluded that this is much more an effect than a true HDR. I believe it belongs with the scene settings such as monochrome and should not be a separate setting. To be blunt, I don't understand why Nikon

Manual Callout

To learn more about the D7100's HDR capabilities, refer to page 115 of your manual.

didn't go the extra mile and add a true HDR button or menu setting that would automate the bracketing process for the user. Instead, the company created a feature that works only with JPEG images and doesn't auto-align. My test results have been mediocre at best, so my recommendation, if you're serious about creating high dynamic range images, is to skip this setting and refer to my steps above.

Chapter 7 Assignments

We've covered a lot of ground in this chapter, so it's time to put our knowledge to work in order to get familiar with these new camera settings and techniques.

Comparing depth of field: wide-angle vs. telephoto

Speaking of depth of field, you should also practice using the hyper focal distance of your lens to maximize the depth of field. You can do this by picking a focal length to work with on your lens.

If you have a zoom lens, try using the longest length. Compose your image and find an object to focus on. Set your aperture to f/22 and take a photo.

Now do the same thing with the zoom lens at its widest focal length. Use the same aperture and focus point.

Review the images and compare the depth of field when using wide angle as opposed to a telephoto lens. Try this again with a large aperture.

Applying hyper focal distance to your landscapes

Pick a scene that once again has objects that are near the camera position and something else that is clearly defined in the background. Try using a wide to medium-wide focal length for this (18–35mm). Use a small aperture and focus on the object in the foreground; then recompose and take a shot.

Without moving the camera position, use the object in the background as your point of focus and take another shot.

Finally, find a point that is one-third of the way into the frame from near to far and use that as the focus point.

Compare all of the images to see which method delivered the greatest range of depth of field from near to infinity.

Using Live View to focus and compose

Now let's get some practice using the rule of thirds for improving composition. To do this, you need to employ Live View with the grid overlay turned on for a little visual assistance.

Using the Live View grid, practice shooting while placing your main subject in one of the intersecting line locations. Take some comparison shots with the subject at one of the intersecting locations, and then shoot the same subject in the middle of the frame.

Get the sharpest image possible by using Live View in conjunction with the Zoom In button. Pan your image using the Multi-selector while zooming in to double-check the sharpness throughout the image.

Placing your horizons

Finally, find a location with a defined horizon and, using the Live View grid, shoot the horizon along the top third of the frame, in the middle of the frame, and along the bottom third of the frame.

Share your results with the book's Flickr group!
Join the group here: flickr.com/groups/nikond7100_fromsnapshotstogreatshots.

8

ISO 160
1/100 sec.
f/14
24mm lens

Mood Lighting

SHOOTING WHEN THE LIGHTS GET LOW

There is no reason to put your camera away when the sun goes down. Your D7100 has some great features that let you work with available light as well as the built-in flash. In this chapter, we will explore ways to push your camera's technology to the limit in order to capture great photos in difficult lighting situations. We will also discuss the use of flash and how best to use your built-in flash features to improve your photography. But let's first look at working with low-level available light.

PORING OVER THE PICTURE

Hands down, one of my favorite destinations for street and cityscape photography is Paris. I can get lost for hours watching people or wandering the streets marveling at the amazing architecture around every corner. Last summer I had the opportunity to take my family there, and while it was supposed to be a family vacation and not a photo trip, they knew I couldn't pass up such great photographic opportunities. I wanted a nice sunset image of the Eiffel Tower, so as we were wandering the streets I was secretly scouting a good location for my image. We finally stumbled upon a beautiful bridge overlooking the Seine River with the Eiffel Tower in the near distance. The final composition was taken from a series of three images over the course of several hours. Did I mention I have a very patient family? I made it up to them with banana-Nutella crepes and an image that will always remind us of our trip to Paris.

As I mentioned in Chapter 7, the golden hour is critical to get that perfect light, so be patient and wait for 30 to 60 minutes after the sun has gone down.

ISO 100
1/30 sec.
f/9
35mm

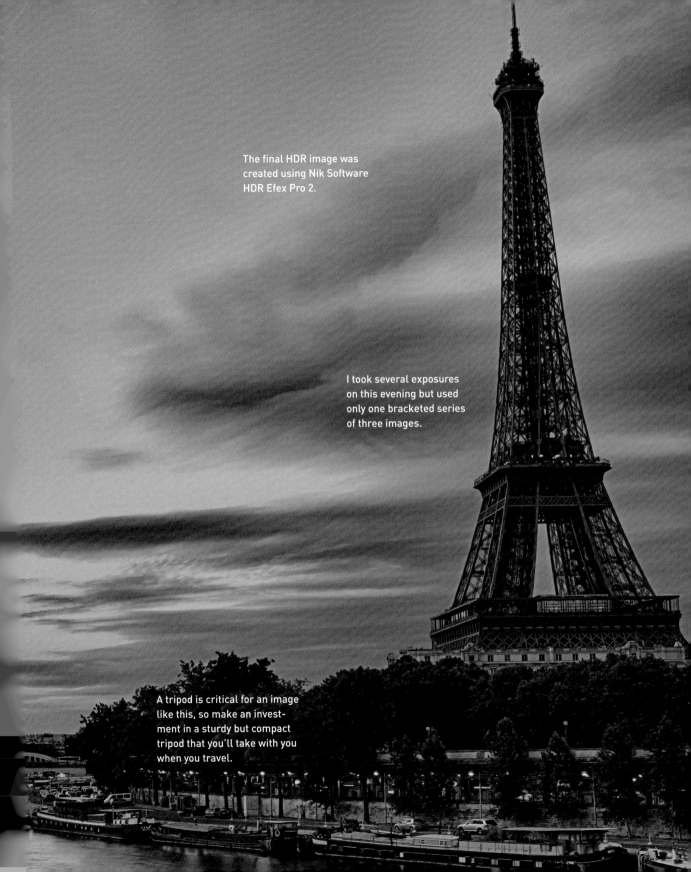

The final HDR image was created using Nik Software HDR Efex Pro 2.

I took several exposures on this evening but used only one bracketed series of three images.

A tripod is critical for an image like this, so make an investment in a sturdy but compact tripod that you'll take with you when you travel.

RAISING THE ISO

Let's begin with the obvious way to keep shooting when the lights get low: raising the ISO (**Figure 8.1**). By now you know how to change the ISO by using the ISO button and the main Command dial. In typical shooting situations, you should keep the ISO in the 100 to 1000 range. This will keep your pictures nice and clean by minimizing the digital noise. But as the available light gets low, you might find yourself working in the higher ranges of the ISO scale, which could lead to more noise in your image. Everyone has a different tolerance for digital noise, so experiment a bit with different ISO settings and see what your limit is. My tolerance depends on my subject. For my landscape photography I have a very low tolerance for digital noise, but for street photography I have been known to let it slide here and there. I think that with most cameras, the digital noise won't become apparent until you exceed 2500 ISO and possibly higher, depending upon the image and conditions.

Now, you could use a flash and try to avoid bumping up your ISO, but that has a limited range of 2 to 28 feet depending upon ISO and aperture settings, which might not work for you. Also, you could be in a situation where flash is prohibited, or at least frowned upon, such as at a play or in a museum.

And what about a tripod in combination with a long shutter speed? That is also an option, and we'll cover it a little later in the chapter. The problem with using a tripod and a slow shutter speed in low-light photography, though, is that it works best when subjects aren't moving. Besides, try to set up a tripod in a museum and see how quickly you grab the attention of the security guards.

So if the only choice for getting the shot is to raise the ISO to 1250 or higher, my recommendation is to consider turning on your High ISO Noise Reduction feature. This custom menu function is set to Off by default, but as you start using higher ISO values you should consider experimenting with the Standard and High settings. Noise is reduced by applying a slight blur to the image, so my suggestion is to experiment with different ISO settings as well as High ISO Noise Reduction strengths to determine what best suits your needs. (Chapter 7 explains how to set the Noise Reduction features.)

Raising Noise Reduction to the Normal setting slightly increases the processing time for your images, so if you are shooting in Continuous Drive mode you might see a little reduction in the speed of your frames per second.

HOT TIP

Don't let digital noise stop you from taking a photo. There are tons of wonderful post-production software programs that help remove digital noise from your image.

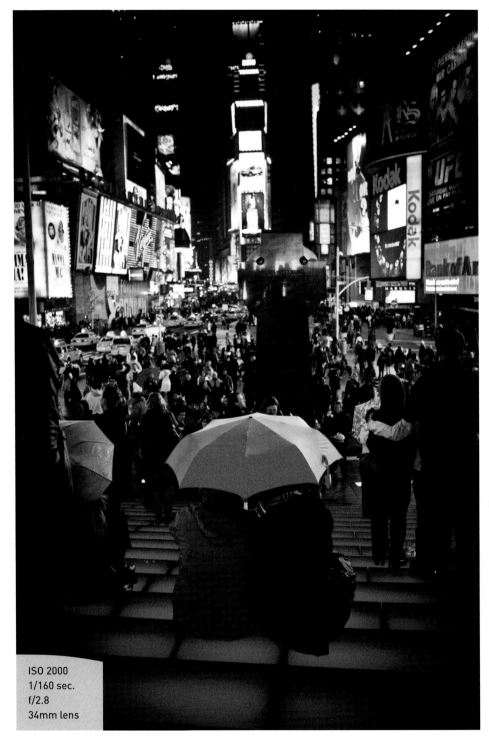

ISO 2000
1/160 sec.
f/2.8
34mm lens

FIGURE 8.1
Wouldn't you know it—the very first time I visited Times Square in New York City it decided to rain. But, the key to good street photography is being able to adapt. I bumped my ISO up to 2000 and got lucky.

NOISE REDUCTION SAVES SPACE

When shooting at very high ISO settings, running High ISO Noise Reduction at the Normal or High setting can save you space on your memory card. If you are saving your photos as JPEGs, the camera will compress the information in the image to take up less space. When you have excessive noise, you can literally add megabytes to the file size. This is because the camera has to deal with more information: It views the noise in the image as photo information and tries not to lose that information during the compression process. Thus, more noise equals bigger files. So not only will turning on the High ISO Noise Reduction feature improve the look of your image, it will also save you some space so you can take a few more shots.

USING VERY HIGH ISOs

Is ISO 6400 just not enough for you? Well, in that case, you will need to set your camera to one of the expanded ISO settings. These settings open up several stops of light as you begin to raise your ISO to the maximum setting of ISO equivalent 25600. The new settings will not appear in your ISO scale as numbers, but as H 0.3 for 8000, H 0.7 for 10000, H 1.0 ISO for 12800, and H 2.0 ISO for 25600.

HOW TO USE THE HIGHER ISO SETTINGS

1. Press and hold the ISO button (**A**). Then rotate the main Command dial while observing the control panel. Rotate the dial until you reach the Hi settings, then release the ISO button.

2. Select H 0.3, H 0.7, H 1.0, or H 2.0 (**B**).

A

B

A word of warning about the expanded ISO settings: Although it is great to have these high ISO settings available during low-light shooting, they should always be your last resort. Even with High ISO Noise Reduction turned on, the amount of visible noise will be extremely high. Try to avoid using high ISO whenever you can, but don't skip an opportunity for a terrific shot because you're afraid to use a higher ISO. The D7100 does remarkably well at 2500 and below, so experiment a little. Remember, a picture never taken is far worse than one with a little noise (**Figure 8.2**)!

ISO 6400
1/160 sec.
f/1.2
85mm lens

FIGURE 8.2
If I hadn't bumped my ISO up to 6400 I would have missed a great memory. Does the image have a little noise? Sure, but I would rather have it than not have the photo!

STABILIZING THE SITUATION

If you purchased your camera with the Vibration Reduction (VR) lens or if you have the kit lens, you already own a great tool to squeeze two stops of exposure out of your camera when shooting without a tripod. The average person can hand-hold a camera down to about 1/60 of a second before blurriness results due to hand shake. Even if you have pipes as big as Mr. T's, you need to use this feature. As the length of the lens is increased (or zoomed), the ability to hand-hold at slow shutter speeds (1/60 and slower) and still get sharp images is further reduced (**Figure 8.3**).

FIGURE 8.3
Turning on the VR switch will allow you to shoot in lower lighting conditions while reducing hand shake. I love this feature—especially if I haven't had my morning coffee.

HANDS OFF FOR SHARPER IMAGES

FIGURE 8.4
A portrait needs to be sharp, and by using the Self-timer, Exposure Delay, or a remote, you reduce the chances of camera shake.

Whether you are shooting with a tripod or even resting your camera on a wall, you can increase the sharpness of your pictures by taking your hands out of the equation. Typically, I like to use a remote shutter release, such as a wireless remote, to avoid placing my hands on the camera, but I've left my remote behind plenty of times. The reality is, whenever you use your finger to depress the shutter release button, you are increasing the chances that there will be a little bit of shake in your image. To eliminate this possibility, try setting your camera up to use the Self-timer or Exposure Delay mode (**Figure 8.4**). We're going to discuss the Self-timer feature, since we've already covered the Exposure Delay mode in Chapter 1.

ISO 500
1/60 sec.
f/11
50mm lens

1. To turn on the Self-timer simply press the Release Mode dial lock and rotate the dial to Self-timer (**A**).

A

2. Press the Menu button to find the Custom Setting Menu. Highlight and select C Timers/AE Lock, then press OK button (**B**).

3. Select C3 Self-timer and click OK button (**C**).

4. Next, highlight Self-Timer Delay and press OK button (**D**).

5. I generally choose 2S (2 seconds) to cut down on time between exposures and reduce my waiting time (**E**).

FOCUSING IN LOW LIGHT

The D7100 has a brand-new focusing system with 51 AF points, but even with this enhancement, on occasion light levels are too low for the camera to achieve an accurate focus. You can do a few things to overcome this obstacle, though.

First, you should know that the camera uses contrast in the viewfinder to establish a point of focus. This is why your camera will not be able to focus when you point it at a white wall or a cloudless sky. It simply can't find any contrast in the scene to work with. Knowing this, you might be able to use a single focus point in AF-S mode to find an area of contrast that is the same distance as your subject. You can then hold that focus by holding down the shutter button halfway and recomposing your image.

Then there are those times when there just isn't anything there for you to focus on. A perfect example of this would be a fireworks display. If you point your lens to the night sky in any AF mode, it will just keep searching for—and not finding—a focus point. On these occasions, you can simply turn off the AF feature and manually focus the lens (**Figures 8.5** and **8.6**). Look for the A/M switch on the side of the lens and slide it to the M position.

FIGURE 8.5
You can't count on autofocus. If the camera just can't find its focus, take it into your own hands.

Now, I don't want any e-mails saying, "John, you broke my camera! It won't focus!" So make sure to switch your lens back to the A mode at the end of your shoot.

FIGURE 8.6
I took this in my field in Montana after watching a magnificent sunset. Autofocus would not work because the light was just too low. I had to switch to manual focus to get the job done.

ISO 200
10 sec.
f/13
70mm lens

AF-ASSIST ILLUMINATOR

I know I told everyone in Chapter 1 that I am not a huge fan of the AF-assist illuminator, but that is primarily when I'm shooting people. The D7100's AF-assist illuminator does a good job helping with focusing by using a small, bright beam from the front of the camera to shine some light on the scene. This light enables the camera to find details to focus on in low-light situations.

This feature is automatically activated when using the flash, except in Landscape, Sports, and Flash Off modes, for the following reasons: In Landscape mode, the subject is usually too far away; in Sports mode, the subject is probably moving; and in Flash Off mode, you've disabled the flash entirely. Also, the illuminator will be disabled when shooting in the AF-C or manual focus mode, as well as when the illuminator is turned off in the camera menu. AF-assist should be enabled by default, but you can check the menu just to make sure.

TURNING ON THE AF-ASSIST FEATURE

1. Press the Menu button and access the Custom Setting Menu. Navigate to the item called A Autofocus and press the OK button on the back of the camera (**A**).

2. Highlight the menu item called A7 Built-in AF-assist Illuminator and press the OK button on the back of the camera (**B**).

3. Set the option to On and press the OK button to complete the setup (**C**).

DISABLING THE FLASH

If you are shooting in one of the automatic scene modes, the flash might be set to activate automatically. If you don't wish to operate the flash, you will have to turn it off in the information screen.

TO TURN OFF FLASH

To disable the flash when shooting in Auto mode, turn the Mode dial to the Flash Off symbol (a circle containing a flash with a slash through it).

Remember, if you are shooting in a professional mode, the only way to get the flash to fire is to turn it on yourself. If you are shooting in an automatic scene mode, depending on the mode, it will come on automatically. For example, in Candlelight and Night Landscape modes, it does not come on, whereas in Pet mode or Night Portrait it is automatically on. If the small flash icon appears on the control panel when you are shooting in a particular mode, it means the setting calls for it and the flash will fire automatically. To turn the flash off in any of the scene modes, simply press the Flash Compensation button at the front of camera while turning the main Command dial until the no flash symbol appears in the control panel.

SHOOTING LONG EXPOSURES

We have covered some of the techniques for shooting in low light, so let's go through the process of capturing a night or low-light scene for maximum image quality (**Figure 8.7**). The first thing to consider is that in order to shoot in low light with a low ISO, you will need to use shutter speeds that are longer than you could possibly hand-hold (longer than 1/15 of a second). This will require the use of a tripod or stable surface for you to place your camera on. For maximum quality, the ISO should be low; I always try to set mine at 100. Consider turning on the Long Exposure Noise Reduction to help minimize any hot pixels. (To set this up, see Chapter 7.)

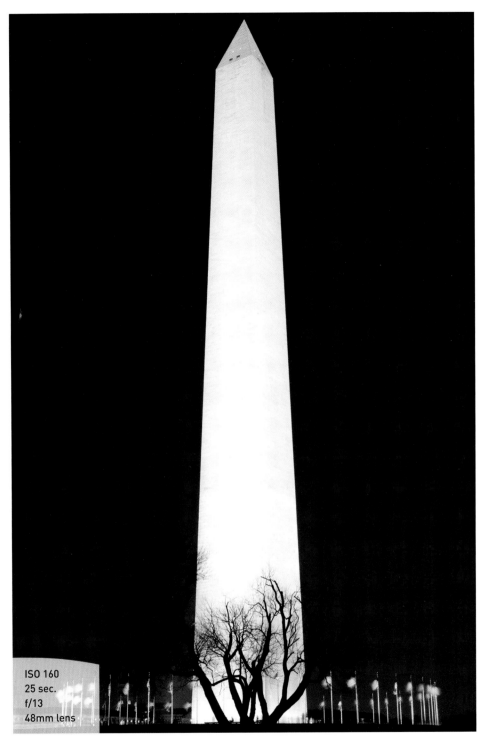

ISO 160
25 sec.
f/13
48mm lens

FIGURE 8.7
This exposure took several tries until I finally got it right. Using a tripod was an absolute must. The longer exposure really helped with silhouetting the tree at the bottom of the frame.

Once you have Noise Reduction turned on, set your camera to Aperture Priority (A) mode. This way, you can concentrate on the aperture that you believe is most appropriate and let the camera determine the best shutter speed. If it is too dark for the autofocus to function properly, try manually focusing. Finally, consider using a cable release or a remote to activate the shutter. If you don't have one, use either the Self-timer mode or Exposure Delay mode (covered later in this chapter and in Chapter 1). Once you shoot the image, you may notice some lag time before it is displayed on the rear LCD. This is due to the noise reduction process, which can take anywhere from a fraction of a second up to 30 seconds, depending on the length of the exposure.

FLASH SYNC

The basic idea behind the term *flash synchronization* (*flash sync* for short) is that when you take a photograph using the flash, the camera needs to ensure that the shutter is fully open at the time that the flash goes off. This is not an issue if you are using a long shutter speed such as 1/15 of a second but does become more critical for fast shutter speeds. To ensure that the flash and shutter are synchronized so that the flash is going off while the shutter is open, the D7100 implements a top sync speed of 1/320 of a second with a compatible flash. This means that when you are using the flash, your shutter speed can't be any faster than 1/320. If you did try to use a faster shutter speed, the shutter would actually start closing before the flash fired, which would cause a black area to appear in the frame where the light from the flash was blocked by the shutter.

USING THE BUILT-IN FLASH

There are going to be times when you have to turn to your camera's built-in flash to get the shot. The pop-up flash on the D7100 is not extremely powerful, but with the camera's advanced metering system, it does a pretty good job of lighting up the night...or just filling in the shadows.

If you are working with one of the automatic scene modes, the flash should automatically activate when needed. If, however, you are working in one of the professional modes, you will have to turn the flash on for yourself. To do this, just press the pop-up flash button located on the front of the camera (**Figure 8.8**). Once the flash is up, it is ready to go. It's that simple.

FIGURE 8.8
A quick press of the pop-up flash button will release the built-in flash to its ready position.

SHUTTER SPEEDS

The standard flash synchronization speed for your camera is between 1/60 and 1/250 of a second. When you are working with the built-in flash in the automatic and scene modes, the camera will typically use a shutter speed of 1/60 of a second. The exception to this is when you use Night Portrait mode, which will fire the flash with a slower shutter speed so that some of the ambient light in the scene has time to record in the image.

The real key to using the flash to get great pictures is to control the shutter speed. The goal is to balance the light from the flash with the existing light so that everything in the picture has an even illumination. Let's take a look at the shutter speeds in the professional modes.

 Programmed (P): The shutter speed stays at 1/60 of a second. The only adjustment you can make in this mode is overexposure or underexposure, using the Exposure Compensation setting or Flash Compensation settings.

 Shutter Priority (S): You can adjust the shutter speed to as fast as 1/250 of a second, all the way down to 30 seconds. The lens aperture will adjust accordingly, but typically at long exposures the lens will be set to its smallest aperture.

 Aperture Priority (A): This mode will allow you to adjust the aperture but will adjust the shutter speed between 1/60 and 1/200 of a second in the standard flash mode.

Because the pop-up flash is fairly small, it does not have enough power to illuminate a large space (**Figure 8.9**). The effective distance varies depending on the ISO setting and aperture. At ISO 200, f/4, the range is about 14 feet. This range can be extended to as far as 20 feet when the camera is set to an ISO of 1600, f/8. For the best image quality, your ISO setting should not go above 1600. Anything higher will begin to introduce excessive noise into your photos. Check out page 123 of your manual for a chart that shows the effective flash range for differing ISO and aperture settings.

FIGURE 8.9
The pop-up flash was used to fill in shadows. The longer exposure time allowed the ambient light to illuminate the rest of the scene.

ISO 400
1/13 sec.
f/3.5
18mm lens

METERING MODES

The built-in flash uses a technology called TTL (Through The Lens) metering to determine the appropriate amount of flash power to output for a good exposure. When you depress the shutter button, the camera quickly adjusts focus while gathering information from the entire scene to measure the amount of ambient light. As you press the shutter button down completely, the flash uses that exposure information and fires a predetermined amount of light at your subject during the exposure.

The default setting for the flash meter mode is TTL. The meter can be set to Manual mode. In Manual flash mode, you can determine how much power you want coming out of the flash ranging from full power all the way down to 1/128 power. Each setting from full power on down will cut the power by half. This is the equivalent of reducing flash exposure by one stop with each power reduction.

SETTING THE FLASH TO THE MANUAL POWER SETTING

1. Press the Menu button and then navigate to the Custom Setting Menu.

2. Using the Multi-selector, highlight the item labeled E Bracketing/Flash and press the OK button (**A**).

3. Highlight item E3 Flash Cntrl for Built-in Flash and press OK (**B**).

4. Change the setting to Manual (**C**) and then press the OK button to adjust the desired power—Full, ½, ¼, and so on—and press the OK button on the back of the camera (**D**).

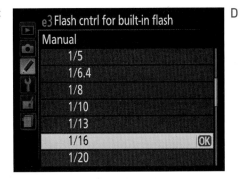

Don't forget to set it back to TTL when you are done because the camera will hold this setting until you change it.

COMPENSATING FOR FLASH EXPOSURE

The TTL system will usually do an excellent job of balancing the flash and ambient light for your exposure, but it does have the limitation of not knowing what effect you want in your image. You may want more or less flash in a particular shot. You can achieve this by using the Flash Compensation feature.

Just as with Exposure Compensation, the Flash Compensation feature allows you to dial in a change in the flash output in increments of 1/3 of a stop. You will probably use this most often to tone down the effects of your flash, especially when you are using the flash as a subtle fill light (**Figures 8.10–8.12**). The range of compensation goes from +1 stop down to –3 stops.

ISO 200
1/100 sec.
f/1.4
85mm lens

FIGURE 8.10
This image was taken with no flash. The exposure is too dark, although we have plenty of detail in highlights.

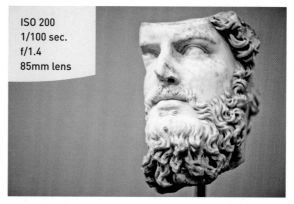

ISO 200
1/100 sec.
f/1.4
85mm lens

FIGURE 8.11
This image was taken using the flash, and now the image appears too light or "blown out." There's very little detail in the highlights.

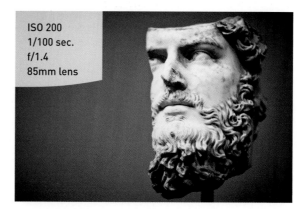

ISO 200
1/100 sec.
f/1.4
85mm lens

FIGURE 8.12
By reducing the flash by one stop, I was able to achieve the exposure I wanted without losing details in the highlights.

1. With the flash in the upright and ready position, press and hold the flash button while viewing the control panel.

2. While holding down the flash button, rotate the Sub-command dial to set the amount of compensation you desire. Turning to the right increases the flash power 1/3 of a stop with each click of the dial. Turning left decreases the flash power. Release the button when you have made your selection.

3. Press the shutter button halfway and then take the picture.

4. Review your image to see if more or less flash compensation is required, and repeat these steps as necessary.

The Flash Compensation feature does not reset itself when the camera is turned off, so whatever compensation you have set will remain in effect until you change it. Your only clue to knowing that the flash output is changed will be the presence of the Flash Compensation symbol in the viewfinder. It will disappear when there is zero compensation set.

REDUCING RED-EYE

We've all seen the result of using on-camera flashes when shooting people: the dreaded red-eye! This demonic effect is the result of the light from the flash entering the pupil and then reflecting back as an eerie red glow. The closer the flash is to the lens, the greater the chance that you will get red-eye. This is especially true when it is dark and the subject's pupils are fully dilated.

There are two ways to combat this problem. The first is to get the flash away from the lens. That's not really an option, though, if you are using the pop-up flash. Therefore, you will need to turn to the Red-eye Reduction feature.

This is a simple feature that shines a light from the camera at the subject, causing his or her pupils to shrink, thus eliminating or reducing the effects of red-eye (**Figure 8.13**).

This small adjustment can make a big difference in time spent post-processing. You don't want to have to go back and remove red-eye from both eyes of every subject!

The feature is set to Off by default and needs to be turned on by using the information screen or by using a combination of the flash button and the main Command dial.

FIGURE 8.13
Notice that the pupils on the image without red-eye are smaller as a result.

ISO 200
1/60 sec.
f/4
22mm lens

TURN ON THE LIGHTS!

When shooting indoors, another way to reduce red-eye, or just shorten the length of time that the reduction lamp needs to be shining into your subject's eyes, is to turn on a lot of lights. The brighter the ambient light levels, the smaller the subject's pupils will be. This will reduce the time necessary for the red-eye reduction lamp to shine. It will also allow you to take more candid pictures because your subjects won't be required to stare at the red-eye lamp while waiting for their pupils to reduce.

TURNING ON THE RED-EYE REDUCTION FEATURE

1. Press and hold the flash button while viewing the control panel.

2. While holding the flash button, rotate the main Command dial until the small eye appears in the box. This means Red-eye Reduction is on. Release the flash button.

3. With Red-eye Reduction activated, compose your photo and then press the shutter release button to take the picture.

When Red-eye Reduction is activated, the camera will not fire the instant that you press the shutter release button. Instead, the Red-eye Reduction lamp will illuminate for a second or two and then fire the flash for the exposure. This is important to remember, as people have a tendency to move around, so you will need to instruct them to hold still for a moment while the lamp works its magic.

Truth be told, I rarely shoot with Red-eye Reduction turned on because of the time it takes before being able to take a picture. If I am after candid shots and have to use the flash, I will take my chances on red-eye and try to fix the problem in my image processing software or even in the camera's retouching menu.

FLASH AND GLASS

If you find yourself in a situation where you want to use your flash to shoot through a window or display case, try placing your lens right against the glass so that the reflection of the flash won't be visible in your image. This is extremely useful in museums and aquariums.

A FEW WORDS ABOUT EXTERNAL FLASH

We have discussed several ways to get control over the built-in pop-up flash on the D7100. The reality is that, as flashes go, it will render only average results. For people photography, it is probably one of the most unflattering light sources that you could ever use. This isn't because the flash isn't good—it's actually very sophisticated for its size. The problem is that light should come from any direction besides the camera to best flatter a human subject. When the light emanates from directly above the lens, it gives the effect of becoming a photocopier. Imagine putting your face down on a scanner: The result would be a flatly lit, featureless photo.

> ## Manual Callout
>
> For more information on the use of external Speedlight flashes on your D7100, check out pages 303–307 of your manual.

To really make your flash photography come alive with possibilities, you should consider buying an external flash such as the Nikon SB-700 AF Speedlight. The SB-700 has a swiveling flash head and more power, and it communicates with the camera and the TTL system to deliver balanced flash exposures.

Chapter 8 Assignments

Now that we have looked at the possibilities of shooting after dark, it's time to put it all to the test. These assignments cover the full range of shooting possibilities, both with flash and without. Let's get started.

How steady are your hands?

It's important to know just what your limits are in terms of handholding your camera and still getting sharp pictures. This will change depending on the focal length of the lens you are working with. Wider angle lenses are more forgiving than telephoto lenses, so check this out for your longest and shortest lenses. Using the 18–55mm zoom as an example, set your lens to 55mm and then, with the camera set to ISO 200 and the mode set to Shutter Priority, turn off the VR and start taking pictures with lower and lower shutter speeds. Review each image on the LCD at a zoomed-in magnification to take note of when you start seeing visible camera shake in your images. It will probably be around 1/60 of a second for a 55mm lens.

Now do the same for the wide-angle setting on the lens. My limit is about 1/30 of a second. These shutter speeds are with the Vibration Reduction feature turned off. If you have a VR lens, try it with and without the VR feature enabled to see just how slow you can set your shutter while getting sharp results.

Pushing your ISO to the extreme

Find a place to shoot where the ambient light level is low. This could be at night or indoors in a darkened room. Using the mode of your choice, start increasing the ISO from 200 until you get to 6400 Hi 1.0. Make sure you evaluate the level of noise in your image, especially in the shadow areas. Only you can decide how much noise is acceptable in your pictures. I can tell you from personal experience that I never like to stray above that ISO 800 mark.

Getting rid of the noise

Turn on High ISO Noise Reduction and repeat the previous assignment. Find your acceptable limits with Noise Reduction turned on. Also pay attention to how much detail is lost in your shadows with this function enabled.

Long exposures in the dark

If you don't have a tripod, find a stable place to set your camera outside and try some long exposures. Set your camera to Aperture Priority mode and then use the Self-timer to activate the camera (this will keep you from shaking the camera while pressing the shutter button).

Shoot in an area that has some level of ambient light, be it a streetlight or traffic lights, or even a full moon. The idea is to get some late-night low-light exposures.

Reducing the noise in your long exposures

Now repeat the last assignment with the Long Exposure Noise Reduction set to On. Look at the difference in the images that were taken before and after Noise Reduction was enabled. For best results, perform this assignment and the previous assignment in the same shooting session using the same subject.

Testing the limits of the pop-up flash

Wait for the lights to get low and then press that pop-up flash button to start using the built-in flash. Try using the different shooting modes to see how they affect your exposures. Use the Flash Exposure Compensation feature to take a series of pictures while adjusting from –3 stops all the way to +1 stop so that you become familiar with how much latitude you will get from this feature.

Getting the red out

Find a friend with some patience and a tolerance for bright lights. Have him or her sit in a darkened room or outside at night and then take a picture with the flash. Now turn on Red-eye Reduction to see if you get better results. Don't forget to have your friend sit still while the red-eye lamp does its thing.

Share your results with the book's Flickr group!
Join the group here: flickr.com/groups/nikond7100_fromsnapshotstogreatshots.

9

ISO 100
1/250 sec.
f/10
80mm lens

Creative Compositions

BETTER PHOTOGRAPHY STARTS
WITH BETTER COMPOSITION

Creating a good image requires you to go beyond your camera settings.
A skilled photographer has an intimate knowledge of his or her camera
capabilities coupled with a sound understanding of composition. Some
people have a natural eye for composition, while others struggle with
how to frame an image. Composition can be taught—I'm proof of that!
This chapter will cover a few of the basic rules of composition and serve
as a nice refresher for the more experienced photographer.

PORING OVER THE PICTURE

To avoid the clutter of the surrounding trees, I used a zoom lens and created a very tight composition.

Including people can add perspective to an image.

ISO 160
1/125 sec.
f/13
140mm lens

Yellowstone National Park's Grand Prismatic Spring is no stranger to photographers, but the trick of making a good photograph is finding an interesting angle. Some of the best images I've seen have been from the air, but because my private helicopter has been in the shop as of late, I had to resort to finding higher ground in the nearby hills. This created a framing challenge, since I had a partially obstructed view due to the nearby trees.

Your eyes are immediately drawn to the brightest part of the image (the blue) and slowly follow the orange streaks of the brightly colored bacteria.

DEPTH OF FIELD

I shoot a majority of my photography using Aperture Priority, and my number one concern beyond how to frame the shot is what depth of field to use. Depth of field can be critical in telling a story. If I want to create a portrait with a blurry background, I use a large or open aperture, such as f/1.2–2.8, to create what we call a shallow depth of field, meaning an in-focus foreground with a blurry background (**Figure 9.1**). If I'm shooting a landscape and the whole scene needs to be sharp, then I'll use a higher or less open aperture, such as f/16, to ensure sharpness.

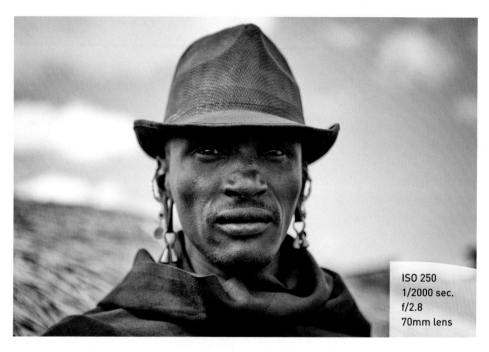

ISO 250
1/2000 sec.
f/2.8
70mm lens

Occasionally a greater depth of field is required to maintain a sharp focus across a farther distance. This might be due to the sheer depth of your subject, where you have objects that are near the camera but sharpness is desired at a greater distance as well (**Figure 9.2**).

Or perhaps you are photographing a reflection. With a shallow depth of field, I could only get the reflected mountains and the mirror in focus. By using a higher aperture, you will be able to maintain acceptable sharpness in both the subject and the reflection (**Figure 9.3**).

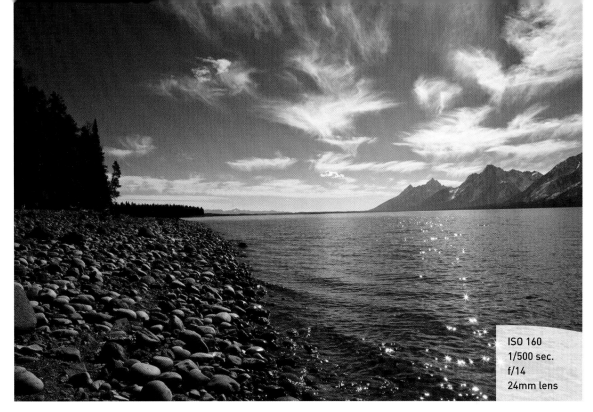

ISO 160
1/500 sec.
f/14
24mm lens

FIGURE 9.2
Typically we want landscape photos to be very sharp, so use a tripod and shoot at a higher aperture to allow for maximum clarity.

ISO 100
1/80 sec.
f/16
24mm lens

FIGURE 9.3
Getting a distant subject in focus in a reflection, along with the reflective surface, requires a small aperture. Keep an eye out for opportunities like this—these are always fun and creative shots.

ANGLES

Having strong angular lines in your image can add to the composition, especially when they are juxtaposed (**Figure 9.4**). This can create a tension that is different from the standard horizontal and vertical lines that we are so accustomed to seeing in photos.

FIGURE 9.4
The strong angular lines of the Louvre made for a dynamic composition.

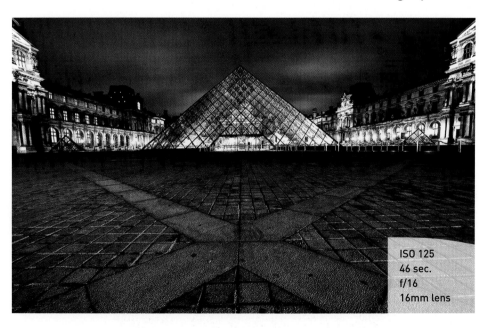

ISO 125
46 sec.
f/16
16mm lens

POINT OF VIEW

Sometimes the easiest way to influence your photograph is to simply change your perspective. Instead of always shooting from a standing position, try moving your camera to a totally different point of view. Try getting down on your knees or even lying on the ground. This low angle can completely change how you view your subject and create a new interest in common subjects (**Figure 9.5**).

ISO 400
1/60 sec.
f/5
18mm lens

FIGURE 9.5
Put your camera in a position that presents an unfamiliar view of your subject or exaggerates an element in the photo. By taking this shot from a low point of view, I exaggerated the height of the man on stilts.

PATTERNS

You can add rhythm and balance to your images by finding the patterns in everyday life and concentrating on the elements that rely on geometric influences. Try to find the balance and patterns that often go unnoticed (**Figure 9.6**).

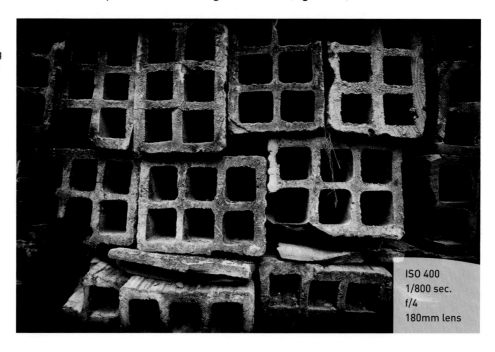

ISO 400
1/800 sec.
f/4
180mm lens

COLOR

Color works well as a tool for composition when you're dealing with very saturated colors. Some of the best colors are those within the primary palette. Reds, greens, and blues, along with their complementary colors (cyan, magenta, and yellow), can all be used to create visual tension (**Figure 9.7**). This tension between bright colors will add visual excitement, drama, and complexity to your images when combined with other compositional elements.

Color can make an image more compelling. I photographed these two Volkswagen bugs in Peru (**Figure 9.8**) partly because the image struck me as comical, but the contrast of the red- and blue-colored cars is really what made the image. Color can add balance, which is pleasing to the eye, or act as a contrast to a subject, adding visual interest.

ISO 125
1/50 sec.
f/10
66mm lens

FIGURE 9.7
Cropping in tight
on this padlock
allowed me to use
the colors as the
primary influ-
ence in the image.
The bright blue is
complemented by
the rusty orange.

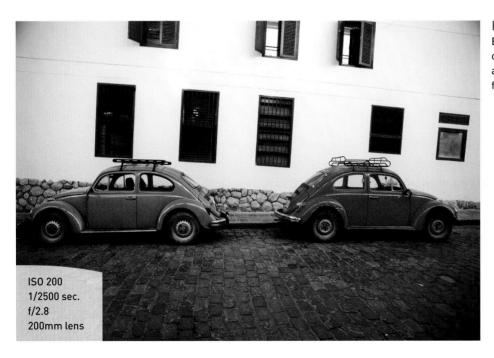

ISO 200
1/2500 sec.
f/2.8
200mm lens

FIGURE 9.8
Bright primary col-
ors playing off one
another can make
for a strong image.

ISO 125
1/640 sec.
f/6.3
16mm lens

FIGURE 9.9
The contrasting colors complement each other and add balance to the scene. This photo was taken with two filters on the camera, and then processed as HDR to really increase the contrast.

CONTRASTING AND COMPLEMENTING

We just saw that you can use color as a strong compositional tool. One of the most effective uses of it is to combine two complementary colors that make the eye move back and forth across the image (**Figure 9.9**). There is no exact combination that will work best, but consider using dark and light colors, or red and green or blue and yellow to provide the strongest visual. Studying a color wheel or color theory can help you to strengthen your color images. (In Figure 9.9, the blue sky and yellow grass are complementary because blue and yellow are across from one another on a color wheel.)

You can also introduce contrast through different geometric shapes that battle (in a good way) for the attention of the viewer. You can combine circles and triangles, ovals and rectangles, curvy and straight, hard and soft, dark and light, and so many more (**Figure 9.10**). You aren't limited to just one contrasting element either. Combining more than one element of contrast will add even more interest. Look for these contrasting combinations whenever you are out shooting, and then use them to shake up your compositions.

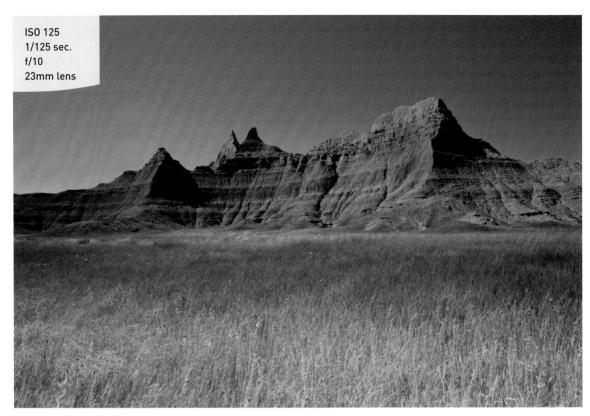

ISO 125
1/125 sec.
f/10
23mm lens

FIGURE 9.10
The angular lines
of the red moun-
tains play against
the green grass
and the perfectly
smooth blue sky to
create contrast with
color and texture.
A gradient filter
was used to increase
the saturation
of the blue sky and
create the shadow
below the mountain.

LEADING LINES

One way to pull a viewer into your image is to incorporate leading lines. These are elements that come from the edge of the frame and then lead into the image toward the main subject. Examples include vanishing perspective lines or an element such as a river—any feature used to move the eye from the outer edge into the heart of the image.

Leading lines can be effective in establishing the mood of an image. Vertical lines feel bold and rigid, while S-curve lines usually give a sense of relaxation or going with the flow. When you're visualizing your image and preparing your composition, remember to be intentional with your composition without losing sight of your creative vision. Leading lines can be particularly striking in black-and-white photography, in which an image's strength rests almost entirely upon its composition (**Figure 9.11**).

FIGURE 9.11
This is a classic
example of a
vanishing point
that is aided by
leading lines.

ISO 200
1/160 sec.
f/8
35mm lens

FIGURE 9.12
I used the rule of thirds to place the lion to the center left of the frame while using negative space to the right side of the frame. This creates a more dynamic and aesthetically appealing portrait. The rule of thirds can be applied to both vertical and horizontal images.

SPLITTING THE FRAME

Generally speaking, splitting the frame right down the middle is not your best option. While it may seem more balanced, it can actually be pretty boring. Consider using the rule of thirds when deciding how to divide your frame (**Figure 9.12**).

When a horizon is in the shot, a low horizon will give a sense of stability to the image. Typically, this is done when the sky is more appealing than the landscape below (**Figure 9.13**). When the emphasis is to be placed on the landscape, the horizon line should be moved upward in the frame, leaving the bottom two-thirds to the subject below.

FIGURE 9.13
I placed the horizon in the bottom third of the frame, with the sky taking up most of the top two-thirds. This helps balance the frame, and also let me capture the active sky. While the barn is in the middle of the frame, the photo remains well balanced from top to bottom because of the use of the rule of thirds.

ISO 100
1/80 sec.
f/10
35mm lens

FIGURE 9.14
By positioning
myself between
the two trees, I was
able to use them as
a frame to empha-
size the barn. It
also gives us a story
about the environ-
ment surrounding
the barn.

FRAMES WITHIN FRAMES

The outer edge of your photograph acts as a frame to hold all of the visual elements of the photograph. One way to add emphasis to your subject is through the use of internal frames (**Figure 9.14**). Depending on how the frame is used, it can create the illusion of a third dimension to your image, giving it a feeling of depth.

Chapter 9 Assignments

Apply the shooting techniques and tools that you have learned in the previous chapters to these assignments, and you'll improve your ability to incorporate good composition into your photos. Make sure you experiment with all the different elements of composition and see how you can combine them to add interest to your images.

Learning to see lines and patterns

Take your camera for a walk around your neighborhood and look for patterns and angles. Don't worry so much about getting great shots as about developing an eye for details.

Point of view

Next time you're out shooting and you see something interesting, force yourself to shoot at least 25 frames of the same subject. Vary your point of view as much as possible. Lie on the ground, climb up high, get close up, get farther away; force yourself to try different points of view. This will train your eye to see these points of view more often. You may be surprised and get an image that you didn't imagine before.

Finding the square peg and the round hole

Circles, squares, and triangles: Spend a few sessions concentrating on shooting simple geometric shapes.

Using the aperture to focus attention

Depth of field plays an important role in defining your images and establishing depth and dimension. Practice shooting wide open, using your largest aperture for the narrowest depth of field. Then find a scene that would benefit from extended depth of field, using very small apertures to give sharpness throughout the scene.

Leading viewers into a frame

Look for scenes where you can use elements as leading lines and then look for framing elements that you can use to isolate your subject and add both depth and dimension to your images.

Share your results with the book's Flickr group!
Join the group here: flickr.com/groups/nikond7100_fromsnapshotstogreatshots.

10

CHASE

CHICAGO

Kiefer

LIGHTS, CAMERA
ACTION!
BY NIKON D7100

ISO 160,
1/100 sec.
f/4.5
85mm lens

Lights, Camera, Action

GETTING THE MOST OUT OF THE D7100'S VIDEO CAPABILITIES

I don't shoot videos professionally, but like many of you I've taken my share of home videos of my family. Once you had to have a camera for your still photos and a camcorder for your video. Well, that's all changed within the last few years, and your D7100 is equipped with amazing video technology. I'm going to cover some of the basics in this chapter to get you started. If you're super serious about video, then I recommend getting your hands on Peachpit's *Creating DSLR Video: From Snapshots to Great Shots.*

RECORDING WITH LIVE VIEW

Video recording is a feature of the Live View capabilities of the camera, so you'll have to put it into active Live View mode to begin capturing video. This is done by rotating the Live View selector to the Movie Live View setting, designated by the Movie camera icon, and pressing the LV button (**Figure 10.1**).

FIGURE 10.1

Rotate the Live View selector to Movie live view.

Next, you need to place the red focus box on the subject and hold down the shutter button halfway until the focusing box turns green, indicating your subject is in focus. Your D7100 continues focusing on your subject when you keep the shutter button pressed down halfway. (Pressing the shutter button down all the way will take a photo as usual, so make sure to press the shutter only halfway when making movies.)

HOLD IT STEADY

I know a lot of people are just going to start shooting video right out of the box without adjusting the settings, so before I move on I have one word of advice: Use a tripod. Have you ever felt like you just finished riding the Cyclone at Coney Island after watching a home video? Handheld video is rough to watch unless the person behind the camera knew what he or she was doing. Buy a tripod or a tripod head that is constructed for video. Typically these tripods will have what's called fluid, smooth, or shake-free panning and tilt features. Trust me, a good investment in a nice tripod for your video will make the difference between professional-looking video and *The Blair Witch Project*.

Once your subject is in focus, you can push the red dot Movie Record button located next to the shutter release button. Use the Movie Record button to start and stop video recording. Remember, in order to record movies you must have Live View activated and Movie Live View selected. As the camera begins to record, you will notice a few new icons on the back LCD. At the top left is a blinking red Record icon to let you know that the camera is in active recording mode. At the upper right, a timer counts down your remaining recording time. The recording time is directly related to the quality of video you have selected as well as the capacity of your memory card. Lower quality video and larger memory cards equal more recording time. The D7100 has a maximum recording time of 20 minutes when set to the High Quality video setting and 29 minutes and 59 seconds when set to the Normal Quality video setting. Keep in mind, these are the maximum times regardless of the size of the memory card. To turn off Movie Live View, make sure you have stopped recording and press the LV button located on the Live View selector. If you wish to use Live View for photography again, then rotate the Live View selector until the camera icon has been selected.

DEDICATING A SECOND CARD TO VIDEO

I'm not a huge fan of having all my video and photos on one SD card because often I'm using two different programs for editing: one for video and one for photos. It's just easier for importing to have one card dedicated to photos and the other to video. Plus, it allows me to dedicate my fastest SD card to video.

TO DEDICATE A VIDEO CARD

1. To assign your video recording to a specific SD card slot, press the Menu button. Use the Multi-selector to highlight Movie Settings, under the Shooting menu, and click the OK button (**A**).

2. Use your Multi-selector to high-light Destination and click the OK button (**B**).

3. Select your desired SD card slot, and press the OK button (**C**).

4. Now your video will be stored to a dedicated card for easier retrieval.

VIDEO QUALITY

The best quality your D7100 is capable of is high-definition video, with a resolution of 1920 x 1080 pixels (aka 1080p). The 1080 represents the height of the video image in pixels, and the *p* stands for progressive, which is the method the camera uses to draw the video on the screen (more on this later). You can select a lower resolution video depending on your needs.

For high-definition television and computer/media-station viewing, you will be best served by using 1920 x 1080. If you plan on recording for the Internet or portable media devices, first check the requirements for uploading to the particular media or devices. Many social sites such as YouTube, Google Plus, and Facebook support HD video, as do the iPad, iPod touch, and competing devices. But before you decide to render HD video, you should know the key benefit of using the lower resolutions: Lower resolution video requires less physical storage due to a smaller pixel count. This means you can fit more video on the storage card, as well as take less time to upload the video to the Internet.

WHAT'S THE DIFFERENCE BETWEEN 1080P AND 1080I?

When it comes to video, two terms describe its quality and how it is captured and displayed on a monitor or screen: progressive and interlaced. Unlike a photo, a video frame is not displayed all at once but instead is drawn sequentially. Interlaced video first draws the odd-numbered lines and then the even-numbered lines. This odd-even drawing is what we sometimes call screen flicker. In progressive video, the type your D7100 produces, the lines are drawn in sequence from top to bottom, usually resulting in better image quality and less screen flicker. For viewing purposes progressive video is preferred, especially with higher definition images.

SETTING MOVIE QUALITY, FRAME SIZE, AND RATE

1. Start by pressing the Menu button. Using your Multi-selector, navigate to the Shooting menu.

2. Using the Multi-selector, highlight Movie Settings and press the OK button (**A**).

3. Highlight Movie Quality and press the OK button (**B**).

4. Select the video quality of your choice and press the OK button (**C**).

5. Now let's set the appropriate frame size and rate (denoted in frames per second) by selecting Frame Size/Frame Rate from the menu and pressing the OK button (**D**).

6. Select your desired frame size and rate (**E**) and press OK button.

7. Your video quality as well as frame size and rate are now set and ready for your use. To change them back, simply follow the previous steps but alter the settings as desired.

HOT TIP

Due to the advances in the D7100 and the removal of the low pass filter (as discussed in the introduction) the camera will create beautiful movies at 1920 x 1080; 30p. For fast-moving subjects such as wildlife, consider a camera setting of 1280 x 720; 60p.

SOUND

The D7100 has made some great strides in providing better audio support than its predecessor. First off, the camera now features a built-in stereo microphone located at the front of the accessory shoe (**Figure 10.2**). This is a big move forward in providing quality sounds. Plus, the camera is equipped to allow both an external mic as well as headphones to be used when recording sound. Now, I'm primarily a still photographer, but I have to tell you: The difference between an external mic and an internal one is night and day. If you're serious about making movies, consider picking up an external mic.

FIGURE 10.2
Make sure the microphone is unobstructed when using it to record sound.

I use a Rode shotgun microphone (**Figure 10.3**) that mounts to the camera's hot shoe and plugs into the stereo audio jack. These mics do a very nice job of recording audio for your videos and are one of the least expensive options.

FIGURE 10.3
The Rode shotgun microphone mounts to the camera's hot shoe and plugs into the stereo audio jack port for recording high-quality sound.

DIALING IN THE MICROPHONE SENSITIVITY

Have you ever noticed when a microphone is just too loud or maybe too soft? I know when I video-conference with my friends and family, sometimes the microphone just isn't picking up my voice very well. The same applies to the D7100 microphone. The cool thing is that Nikon did a great job of allowing you to dial in the exact settings you want for the microphone's sensitivity to sounds. By default the microphone is set to Auto Sensitivity, but let's review how we can make manual adjustments.

1. Following the directions for setting Movie Quality, above, locate the Movie Settings menu and press the OK button.

2. Highlight Microphone and press OK again (**A**).

3. Select Manual Sensitivity and press OK (**B**).

A

4. Now, using your Multi-selector, move up to increase or down to decrease sound sensitivity and press OK (**C**).

5. Press the Menu button twice or the LV button to return to Shooting mode.

6. I recommend checking your sound adjustments to make sure you're happy with your results. Remember, you can always set the microphone back to Auto Sensitivity by using the previous steps and selecting Auto instead of Manual.

B

C

TURNING OFF THE SOUND

Sometimes you may wish to turn the sound off altogether—maybe sound would be distracting or you plan on adding your own soundtrack later. This comes in handy when I add the *Chariots of Fire* soundtrack to my daughter's cross-country videos.

TO TURN OFF SOUND

1. Following the directions for setting Movie Quality, above, locate the Movie Settings menu and press the OK button.

2. Highlight Microphone and press OK again (**A**).

3. Select the Microphone Off option and press OK to lock in the change (**B**).

4. Press the Menu button twice or the LV button to return to Shooting mode.

A

B

PLAYBACK

You have a couple of options for reviewing your video once you have finished recording. The first, and probably the easiest, is to press the Image Review button to bring up the recorded image on the rear LCD, and then use the OK button to start playing the video. The Multi-selector acts as the video controller and allows you to rewind and fast-forward as well as stop the video altogether (see page 171 of your manual for more information).

If you would like to watch your high-definition video on your television, then you will need to buy an HDMI cable (your TV must support at least 720HD and have an HDMI port to use this option). Plug the HDMI cable into your television and the other end of the cable into your camera's HDMI port (**Figure 10.4**). Once you have the cable hooked up, simply use the same camera controls that you use for watching the video on the rear LCD.

If you want to watch your high-definition video on your computer, you have two options. If your computer has an HDMI port, then simply plug the cable into your camera and the computer's HDMI port and off you go. Or use my preferred method of simply importing the file to your computer using a host program like Adobe Lightroom, Aperture, or Nikon's NX2, which came with your camera. The video file will have the extension .mov at the end of the filename. These files should play on either a Mac or a PC using software that came with your operating system (QuickTime for Mac and Windows Media Player for PC).

FIGURE 10.4
Plug your cable into this port to watch videos on your television.

FOCUSING

Your D7100 has given you several focusing options for Live View/Movie mode. There are benefits to each focus-point option. You can choose Face-priority AF, Wide-area AF, Normal-area AF, and Subject-tracking AF. You will want to choose your focus mode depending on the subject of your video. Face-priority will search for faces within the frame and place a box

Manual Callout

See pages 155 to 156 in your manual for more details on the AF-area modes.

around each face. When you depress the shutter button halfway, the box will turn from red to green once the face is in focus. This is one of the slower focusing modes, so if you have a fast-moving subject, this may not be your first choice. If you want to follow your subject through the frame and keep that person's face in focus at all times, Subject-tracking AF would be a good option. Wide-area AF and Normal-area AF allow you to choose the subject that you want to focus on. Wide-area provides a larger focusing area than Normal-area AF. Again, the box surrounding your focus point will turn green when the subject is in focus.

TO SELECT YOUR AUTOFOCUS MODE FOR VIDEO

1. Activate Live View by pressing the LV button. Next, Press the AF mode button (**A**) and rotate the Sub-command dial to the desired AF-area mode (**B**).

2. Point your camera at a person and watch as the yellow frame appears over the face in the LCD and press the shutter to begin focus (**C**).

3. Press the red Movie Record button to begin recording the movie.

EDITING

You can do limited editing with Nikon's Movie Editor, which came with your Nikon View NX2 installation CD. This is a great way to do some quick editing without spending money on external software.

If you are serious about editing your videos, I recommend checking out Apple's Final Cut Express or Adobe's Premiere Elements. Both of these software packages will give you excellent control as well as more options for video editing.

Chapter 10 Assignments

Hold it steady

Shoot a video where you are handholding the camera to the best of your abilities. Now practice with the camera on a tripod. Play back the videos and look for differences in ease of viewing.

Video quality

Shoot video using both the highest quality setting and the lowest quality setting. Then, view your video on the LCD on the back of the camera. Watch to see the difference in the HD quality video versus the lower quality. Also note the difference in how much space was used on your memory card between the two videos. Now, connect your camera to your TV and watch the videos. If you have HDMI cable and a high-definition TV, you will see what a drastic difference the quality makes. Once you see the difference, you will know when you want to use lower quality video versus the highest quality.

Share your results with the book's Flickr group!
Join the group here: flickr.com/groups/nikond7100_fromsnapshotstogreatshots.

11

ISO 200
1/320 sec.
f/9
200mm lens

Advanced Techniques

IMPRESS YOUR FAMILY AND FRIENDS

We've covered a lot of ground in the previous chapters, especially on the general photographic concepts that apply to most, if not all, shooting situations. There are, however, some specific tools and techniques in this chapter that will give you an added advantage in obtaining a great shot. Additionally, we will look at how to customize certain controls on your camera to reflect your personal shooting preferences so you will always have them at the ready.

A tripod and cable release (or remote) are a must whenever you're taking a long exposure.

Using a wide-angle lens low to the ground allowed me to create a unique perspective.

A four-stop ND filter allowed me to take a long exposure and create a smoothing effect on the water and clouds.

ISO 100
45 sec.
f/22
16mm lens

Using a high f-stop assisted in creating a sharp focus throughout the entire scene.

Ireland was always on my wish list of places to visit, and just last year my dream came true as I traveled across the beautiful countryside. Amazing landscapes greeted me at nearly every stop on what ended up being a harrowing trip, as I learned to drive on the opposite side of the road. The Dingle was especially beautiful, and when the tide is out seaweed-covered rocks dot the coastline, waiting patiently for the sea to return.

SPOT METER FOR MORE EXPOSURE CONTROL

Generally speaking, Matrix Metering mode provides accurate metering information for the majority of your photography. It does an excellent job of evaluating the scene and then relating the proper exposure information to you. The only problem with this mode is that, like any metering mode on the camera, it doesn't know what it is looking at. In specific circumstances, you'll want to get an accurate reading from just a portion of a scene and discount all of the remaining area in the viewfinder. To give you greater control of the metering operation, you can switch the camera to Spot Metering mode. This allows you to take a meter reading from a very small circle in the center of the viewfinder, while ignoring the rest of the viewfinder area.

So when would you need to use this? Think of a person standing in front of a very dark wall. In Matrix Metering mode, the camera would see the entire scene and try to adjust the exposure information so that the dark background is exposed to render a lighter wall in your image. This means that the scene would actually be overexposed and your subject would then appear too light. To correct this, you can place the camera in Spot Metering mode and take a meter reading right off of—and *only* off of—your subject, ignoring the dark wall altogether. Spot Metering will read the location where you have your focus point, placing all of the exposure information right on your point of interest.

Other situations that would benefit from Spot Metering mode include:

- Snow or beach environments where the overall brightness level of the scene could fool the meter (**Figure 11.1**)
- Strongly backlit subjects that leave the subject underexposed
- Cases where the overall feel of a photo is too light or too dark

SETTING UP AND SHOOTING IN SPOT METERING MODE

1. Make sure the camera is in one of the professional shooting modes, as indicated by M, A, S, or P on the Mode dial. You cannot change metering in the automatic modes.
2. Press and hold the Metering button while rotating the main Command dial with your thumb. Select Spot Metering by watching the control panel as you turn the Command dial.
3. Once you have selected Spot Metering, release the meter button.
4. Now use the Multi-selector to move the focus point onto your subject and take your photo. The meter reading will come directly from the location of the focus point.

ISO 200
1/250 sec.
f/14
16mm lens

FIGURE 11.1
Snowy images can be extremely difficult to expose correctly, so I'll often use Spot Metering, like I did with this image. Knowing that the sky was probably going to be blown out, I took a meter reading off the water. Later I converted this image to black and white, something I frequently do with images featuring snow.

Note that if you are using the Auto-area AF mode, the camera will use the center focus point as the Spot Metering location.

When using Spot Metering mode, remember that the meter believes it is looking at a middle gray value, so you might need to incorporate some exposure compensation of your own to the reading that you are getting from your subject. This will come from experience as you use the meter.

METERING FOR SUNRISE OR SUNSET

Capturing a beautiful sunrise or sunset is all about the sky. If there is too much foreground in the viewfinder, the camera's meter will deliver an exposure setting that is accurate for the darker foreground areas while leaving the sky overexposed, undersaturated, and generally not very compelling (**Figure 11.2**). To gain more emphasis on the colorful sky, point your camera at the brightest part of it and take your meter reading there. Use the AE Lock to meter for the brightest part of the sky and then recompose. The result will be an exposure setting that underexposes the foreground but provides a darker, more dramatic sky (**Figure 11.3**).

FIGURE 11.2
Where you meter can affect the mood and overall quality of your image. Originally, I metered off the rower, which exposed the foreground properly but lost contrast and detail in the sky.

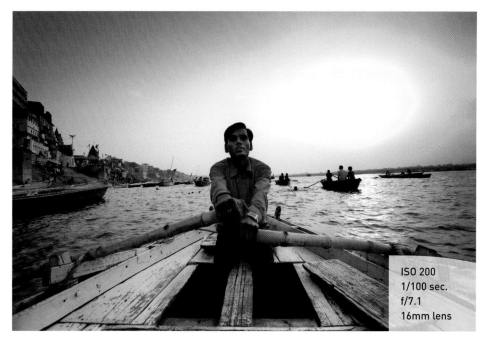

ISO 200
1/100 sec.
f/7.1
16mm lens

FIGURE 11.3
By taking the meter reading from the brightest part of the sky, I got a darker, more colorful sunset. You can still see detail in the man and the boat, but the beautiful sunset is more colorful and dramatic.

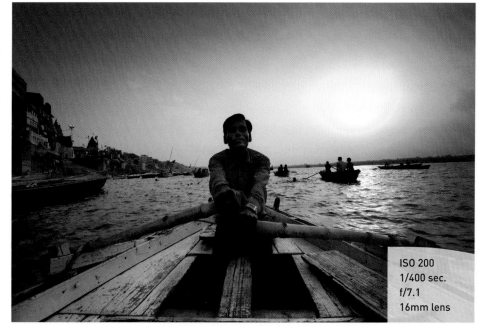

ISO 200
1/400 sec.
f/7.1
16mm lens

MANUAL MODE

Probably one of the most advanced skills to master is shooting in Manual mode. With the power and utility of most of the automatic modes, Manual mode almost never sees the light of day. I have to admit that I don't use it very often, but at times no other mode will do. One of the situations that works well with Manual is studio work with external flashes. When I work with studio lights, my exposure will not change, so I use Manual to eliminate any automatic changes that might happen from shooting in Program, Shutter Priority, or Aperture Priority mode.

This image (**Figure 11.4**) was taken at my studio using a simple portable shooting table and two external flashes. One flash was used underneath the transparent table and the other flash was used with a small soft box. Manual mode allowed me to avoid changes in my setup.

Since I knew the light was a constant, it allowed me to take the time to make adjustments manually to expose the image exactly how I wanted it. Manual mode gives you ultimate creative control.

FIGURE 11.4
These tulips provided a nice subject for a studio still life. In order to expose the flowers correctly and get the look I wanted, I used Manual mode.

ISO 100
1/100 sec
f/18
80mm lens

BULB PHOTOGRAPHY

If you want to work with long shutter speeds that don't quite fit into one of the selectable shutter speeds, you can choose Bulb. This setting is available only in Manual mode, and its sole purpose is to open the shutter at your command and then close it again when you decide to. Several scenarios where you would want to use Bulb mode come to mind: shooting fireworks, photographing lightning, capturing the movement of the stars at night (star trails), or any other very long exposure.

If you are photographing fireworks, you could certainly use one of the longer shutter speeds available in Shutter Priority mode, since they are available for exposure times up to 30 seconds—but many long exposures require shutter speeds much longer than 30 seconds.

Star trail photography is one of my favorite techniques to teach at my Death Valley workshop, because the skies are typically very clear with little light pollution (**Figure 11.5**). The key to successfully shooting any bulb exposure, and especially star trail photography, is setting your camera to Bulb mode while using a tripod and a locking cable release. It's not uncommon for a star trail exposure to take several minutes to several hours, so be patient. Here are some tips that will help you explore your camera's Bulb setting while capturing star trails.

- Set the camera to Bulb mode.

- Use a low ISO (I used 200).

- Use a fairly open aperture (I used f/4).

- Use a wide-angle lens (18mm for your kit lens).

- Locate the North Star, Polaris.

- Focus your lens to infinity while pointing to Polaris. Remember to turn autofocus off!

- Make sure your D7100 batteries are fully charged!

- Feel free to skip Mirror Up Mode (for exposures of 30 seconds or longer Mirror Lockup is really not needed).

- Use a locking cable release.

- Exposure: This is where the real art comes in. For a half moon or brighter, you'll want to start at around 15 minutes. If no moon exists or if you have a new moon, you'll be looking at from upwards of 50 minutes to two hours. The longer the exposure, the longer the star trails will be, which is why you want to try to plan for a new-moon phase.

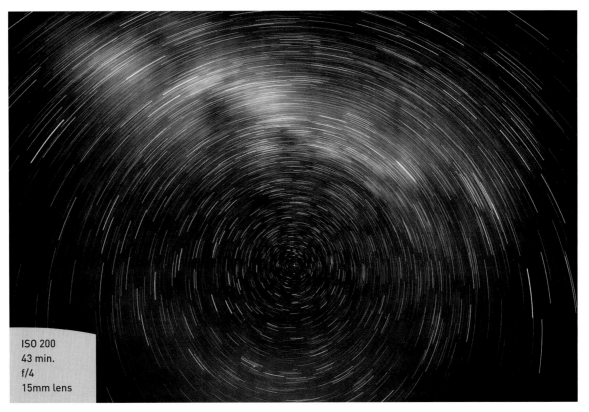

ISO 200
43 min.
f/4
15mm lens

To select the Bulb setting, simply place your camera in Manual mode, press the shutter release halfway to activate metering, and then rotate the main Command dial to the left until the shutter speed displays Bulb on the control panel.

When you're using the Bulb setting, the shutter will stay open only while you are holding down the shutter button. You should also be using a sturdy tripod or shooting surface to eliminate any self-induced vibration while using the Bulb setting. Pressing the shutter button down opens the shutter, and releasing it closes the shutter.

I want to point out that using your finger on the shutter button for a Bulb exposure will definitely increase the chances of getting some camera shake in your images. To get the most benefit from Bulb, I suggest using a remote cord such as the Nikon MC-DC2 Remote Switch, Nikon ML-L3, or WR-R10 Wireless Remote. For more information on using Bulb exposures with the different Nikon remotes, see pages 130 and 310 in the manual. You may want to turn on Long Exposure Noise Reduction (aka Long Exp. NR), as covered in Chapter 8, but remember, the time for your camera to process that image nearly equals that of the exposure itself.

FIGURE 11.5
Stair trail photography requires a very clear night sky and a lot of patience!

AVOIDING LENS FLARE

Lens flare is one of the problems you will encounter when shooting in bright sunlight. Lens flare will show itself as bright circles on the image (**Figure 11.6**). Often you will see multiple circles in a line leading from a very bright light source, such as the sun. The flare is a result of the sun bouncing off the multiple pieces of optical glass in the lens and then being reflected back onto the sensor. You can avoid the problem using one of these methods:

- Try to shoot with the sun coming from over your shoulder, not in front of you or in your scene.

- Use a lens shade to block the unwanted light from striking the lens. You don't have to have the sun in your viewfinder for lens flare to be an issue. All the sunlight has to do is strike the front glass of the lens to make flare happen.

- If you don't have a lens shade (hood), try using your hand or some other element to block the light.

FIGURE 11.6
I shoot a lot of images with sunbursts, and one of the problems I deal with is flare spots. These spots are visible as small circles of light coming down from the sun. While some like this look on occasion, you will want to know how to shoot in the sun without flare as well.

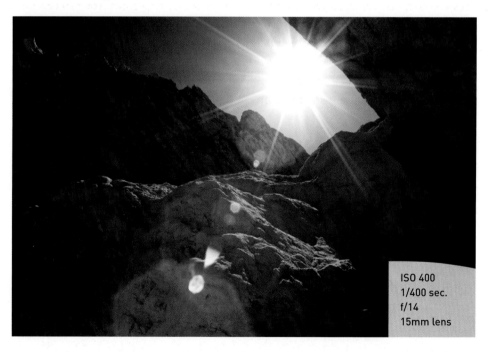

ISO 400
1/400 sec.
f/14
15mm lens

BRACKETING EXPOSURES

So, what if you are doing everything right in terms of metering and mode selection, yet your images still sometimes come out too light or too dark? A technique called bracketing will help you find the best exposure value for your scene by taking a normal exposure as well as one that is over- and underexposed. Having these differing exposure values will most often present you with one frame that just looks better than the others.

If I am in a tricky situation when I have to get the exposure right, such as an outdoor wedding, then I'll use bracketing. I'll start by spacing my exposures apart by one stop and taking three images: one normal exposure, one underexposure, and one overexposure. This is exactly the same technique we use in Chapter 7 for HDR (**Figure 11.7**).

As you are viewing the control panel and holding the exposure button, you can decide how much variation you want between bracketed exposures. You can choose from one-third of a stop all the way to three full stops of exposure difference between each bracketed exposure. If I am in a particularly difficult setting, I will typically bracket in two-stop increments to help zero in on that perfect exposure, and then just delete the ones that didn't make the grade (**Figures 11.8–11.10**). Remember, your lighting will dictate how many stops you want between exposures.

FIGURE 11.7
The control panel shows you just how much bracketing is being applied on an over/under scale in the upper right corner of the screen. The number and letter to the left tell you how many frames you're shooting; here, it's three frames, shown as 3F.

ISO 800
1/20 sec.
f/3.5
16mm lens

FIGURE 11.8
Two stops of exposure below normal, creating a much darker image.

FIGURE 11.9
Normal exposure,
as indicated by the
camera meter.

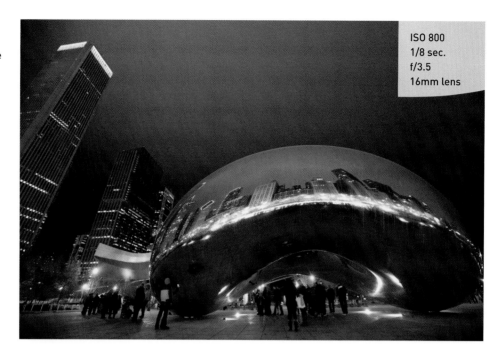

ISO 800
1/8 sec.
f/3.5
16mm lens

FIGURE 11.10
Two stops of expo-
sure above normal,
creating a much
lighter image.

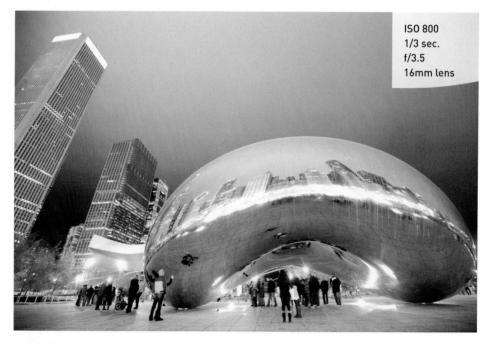

ISO 800
1/3 sec.
f/3.5
16mm lens

SETTING AUTO-EXPOSURE BRACKETING

1. You can quickly set your bracketing by holding down the BKT button (on the front of your camera, directly below the flash button) while rotating the main Command dial to 3F (three frames, or exposures).

2. Next, continue holding your BKT button down while rotating your Sub-command dial to the 2.0 setting (two stops between each exposure). For more information on bracketing, please review pages 133–134 of your manual.

3. If you are in Single Frame shooting mode, you will have to press the shutter three times, one for each exposure. If you are in continuous shooting mode, you will press and hold the shutter button and the camera will take all three exposures with one press of the button.

When I am out shooting in the RAW file format, I typically shoot with my camera set to an exposure compensation of –1/3 stop to protect my highlights. If I am dealing with a subject that has a lot of different tonal ranges from bright to dark, I will often bracket by one stop over and one stop under my already compensated exposure. That means I will have exposures of –1 1/3, –1/3, and +2/3.

Another thing to remember is that auto-exposure bracketing will use the current mode for making exposure changes. This means that if you are in Aperture Priority mode, the camera will make adjustments to your shutter speed. Likewise, if you are in Shutter Priority, the changes will be made to your aperture value. This is important to keep in mind because it could affect certain aspects of your exposure, such as depth of field or camera shake. You also need to know that AE bracketing will remain in effect until you set it back to zero, even if you turn the camera off and then on again.

MACRO PHOTOGRAPHY

Put simply, macro photography is close-up photography. Depending on the lens or lenses that you got with your camera, you may have the perfect tool for macro work. Some lenses are designed to shoot in a macro mode, but you don't have to feel left out if you don't have one of those. Check the spec sheet that came with your lens to see what its minimum focusing distance is.

ISO 100
1/80 sec.
f/18
80mm lens

FIGURE 11.11

A good macro shot is all about details. I want you to meet my very own lady slipper orchid, which I've been nursing along for more than two years since her last bloom. Using a low ISO, high f-stop, and Live View allowed me to capture the great details of the bloom.

If you have a zoom, you should work with the lens at its longest focal length. Also, work with a tripod because handholding will make focusing difficult. The easiest way to make sure that your focus is precisely where you want it to be is to use manual focus mode with the aid of Live View. Live View is very handy in allowing you to zoom in on an object and carefully fine-tune your focus.

I also recommend using A (Aperture Priority) mode so that you can achieve differing levels of depth of field. Long lenses at close range can make for very shallow depth of field, so you will need to work with apertures that are probably much smaller than you would normally use. If you are shooting outside, try shading the subject from direct sunlight by using some sort of diffusion material, such as a white sheet or a diffusion panel. By diffusing the light, you will see much greater detail because you will have a lower contrast ratio (softer shadows), and detail is often what macro photography is all about (**Figure 11.11**).

ACTIVE D-LIGHTING

Your camera provides a function that can automatically make your pictures look better: Active D-Lighting. It works this way: The camera evaluates the tones in your image and then underexposes for the highlight areas while lightening any areas that it believes are too dark or lacking in contrast (**Figures 11.12** and **11.13**). Active D-Lighting is automatically applied to images that are shot in any of the automatic scene modes except for High Key, Low Key, and Silhouette.

You can choose from six levels: Off, Low (L), Normal (N), High (H), Extra High (H*), and Auto (A). You will need to evaluate the strength of the effect on your images and change the level accordingly. I typically leave it set to Normal so that I have brighter, more detailed shadow areas in my photographs while still maintaining good exposure in my skies. You should know that Active D-Lighting can only be adjusted when you are using one of the professional modes. Also, you will want to turn it off if you are using flash exposure compensation because it will work against you when you alter the flash strength.

ISO 160
1/60 sec.
f/5.6
32mm lens

FIGURE 11.12
Without Active D-Lighting, the shadows are very dark and lack contrast.

ISO 160
1/60 sec.
f/5.6
32mm lens

FIGURE 11.13
With D-Lighting set to Normal, you will see shadows become lighter. Notice how we can see more detail in the vendor's face and within the booth.

SETTING UP ACTIVE D-LIGHTING

1. Press the I button to activate the cursor in the information screen, then navigate to the Active D-Lighting setting by using the Multi-selector (**A**).

2. Press the OK button and then move the Multi-selector up or down to select the level of Active D-Lighting that you desire (**B**).

3. Press the OK button to lock in your changes and resume shooting.

The Active D-Lighting setting can also be changed in the Shooting menu.

A

B

CONCLUSION

As my mother used to say, "You'll never be content doing something you don't enjoy." You may have noticed I quote my mom a lot—she was a wise lady! Photography has always been an enjoyable outlet for me. My photographic journey has been filled with its share of mistakes. The learning curve can be steep, so don't beat yourself up as you're learning a new camera. It all takes time, and you're taking the right steps by doing research like reading this book to guide you along in your journey.

We've covered a lot of ground over these last few chapters, and not everything is going to sink in overnight. After all, it took me 20-plus years to learn it! Take a breather, do the practice assignments at the end of the chapters, reflect upon your progress, and most importantly, remember what Mom said: "Enjoy."

The reality is, mastering a skill takes time. I have over 150,000 images to my name. Steve McCurry has over 1,000,0000. The bottom line is, the more you shoot, the better you'll be at your craft. Who knows, maybe one day your hobby will become your full-time job, or maybe you'll even be the next Henri Cartier-Bresson. The main thing to remember is, all photographers start at the same point, but one thing all the greats have in common is they know their equipment inside and out. I hope you enjoy your new D7100, and I can't wait to see your photographic journey on our Flickr group.

Chapter 11 Assignments

Many of the techniques covered in this chapter are specific to shooting situations that may not come about very often. That doesn't mean you shouldn't learn them. Play around with them, and then when the situation does present itself you will be ready.

Adding some drama to the end of the day

Most sunset photos don't reflect what the photographer saw because he or she didn't meter correctly for them. The next time you see a colorful sunset, pull out your camera and take a meter reading from the sky, then one without the sky, and see what a difference it makes.

Making your exposure spot on

Using the Spot Metering mode can give accurate results, but only when the meter is pointed at something that has a middle tone. Try adding something gray to the scene and taking a reading off it. Now switch back to your regular meter mode and see if the exposure isn't slightly different.

Using the Bulb setting to capture the moment

This is definitely one of those settings that you won't use often, but it's pretty handy when you need it. If you have the opportunity to shoot a fireworks display, distant storm, or even a star trail, try setting the camera to Bulb and varying the length of the exposure until you get the results you want.

Bracketing your way to better exposures

Why settle for just one variation of an image when you can bracket to get the best exposure choice? Set your camera up for a 3 Frame bracket series and then expand your exposure by one stop so that in the end you have -1, 0, and +1 exposures. This is a great tool in helping you to understand exposure compensation, which we discussed in Chapter 7.

Moving in for a close-up

Macro photography is best practiced on stationary subjects, which is why I like flowers. If you have a zoom lens, check the minimum focusing distance and then try to get right to that spot to squeeze the most from your subject. Try using a diffuse light source as well to minimize shadows.

Share your results with the book's Flickr group!
Join the group here: flickr.com/groups/nikond7100_fromsnapshotstogreatshots.

INDEX

S

microphone for, 240–241

quality settings for, 238–239, 245

reviewing recorded video, 242–243

sound settings for, 242

starting/stopping, 236

time limits for, 236–237

viewfinder grid display, 22, 184–185

W

warm colors, 176

water, flowing, 87, 89, 90, 180–181

WB button, 8, 170

white balance settings, 6–8

assignment on using, 25

choices available for, 7

custom presets for, 170–171

landscape photography and, 168–171

Live View feature and, 170

RAW file format and, 6

scene modes and, 74

steps for selecting, 8

wide-angle lenses, 41–42

depth of field and, 42, 138

distortion caused by, 41, 138, 150

portraits and, 138, 150, 151

wildlife photography, 44, 92

wireless remote, 255

Z

zoo photography, 96

Zoom In/Out buttons, 112

zoom lenses, 44, 95

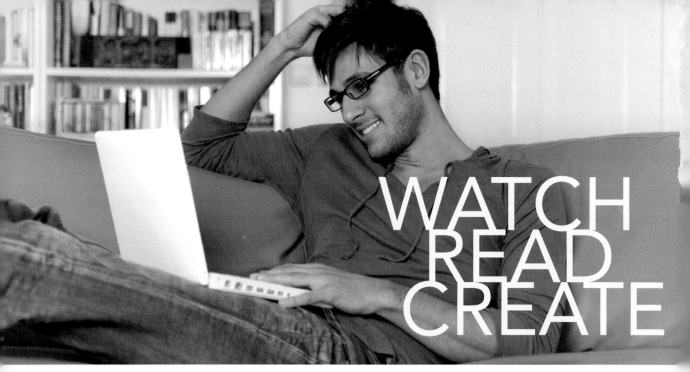

WATCH READ CREATE

Unlimited online access to all Peachpit, Adobe Press, Apple Training and New Riders videos and books, as well as content from other leading publishers including: O'Reilly Media, Focal Press, Sams, Que, Total Training, John Wiley & Sons, Course Technology PTR, Class on Demand, VTC and more.

No time commitment or contract required! Sign up for one month or a year. All for $19.99 a month

SIGN UP TODAY
peachpit.com/creativeedge